In *Both*, Noel invites us to tag da and red-light districts of Th Ukraine. This journey will forever challenge the way you think about missions and help you live out your faith in a fresh, new way.

Bob Goff
Speaker, coach, author of *New York Times* best-selling books, *Love Does* and *Everybody Always*

For over a decade, I've served alongside Noel in some of the most brutal yet beautiful, gritty but grace-filled places around the world. In every situation, Noel has been the strong, compassionate voice that boldly speaks for those who cannot speak for themselves. In *Both*, the help and hope Noel brings through her life-changing work springs off the pages through her perspective-shifting words. I urge every Christian to sit with Noel as she broadens our minds and deepens our hearts for Jesus and a hurting world. Our lives and our purpose must be motivated by Both.

Lori Wilhite
Founder of Leading and Loving It, author of *Philippians: Chasing Happy*

Noel Brewer Yeatts walks the talk. I know because I've walked a few steps with her on her long, arduous journey of living out her faith across the globe to serve "the least of these." In *Both*, Noel offers a much-needed challenge to the church: we must not choose between body and soul or between faith and works. The Christian is called to serve both and embody both. Noel's life, ministry, and words challenge and convict me. And they give me hope that by being the body of Christ, we can serve other bodies—and their souls, too.

Karen Swallow Prior, Ph.D.
Author of *The Evangelical Imagination: How Stories, Images & Metaphors Created a Culture in Crisis*

Both is a message we desperately need today. Noel offers a fresh perspective for how faith reveals itself in love. She brilliantly shows how the good news is good, both for us and for the world.

Jud Wilhite
Senior pastor of Central Church, Las Vegas, Nevada; author of *Pursued*

Some leaders challenge you to think. Some leaders inspire you to take action. Noel Yeatts is the rare leader who does both. Her new book, *Both: Living Outside the Either/Or of Your Faith*, will challenge your perspective on missions and inspire you to believe that both help AND hope are possible.

Jenni Catron
Author, speaker, leadership & culture consultant

Noel Yeatts has given us a gift: a guidebook to change the world. Christian compassion gives hope because it brings help, spiritual and physical help.

Rev. Johnnie Moore
Author, *The New Book of Christian Martyrs*
President, The Congress of Christian Leaders

Noel Yeatts issues a profound call to believers everywhere to awaken to the spiritual and physical needs of those around the world. She challenges us to rethink what missions looks like and recognize love is an action. You'll find your heart set on fire through these pages.

Margaret Feinberg
Author of *More Power To You*

Noel Yeatts has written for all of us, a very challenging book that will cause you to never look at "missions" the same way again. With fantastic stories and illustrations, she vividly paints a new picture for what our daily lives should look like as faithful believers. This book will radically change the way you see mission work, and it has the potential to change your life.

Charles Billingsley
Concert artist/worship leader - Teaching pastor, Thomas Road Baptist Church, Lynchburg, Virginia

I've been in ministry for over three decades, and Noel's reframing of the term "mission work" has greatly impacted my life and my ministry. She so beautifully marries the call of Christians to share the Gospel of Jesus AND to help meet life's basic needs like food and clean water. Partnering with Noel and World Help was the obvious choice for our Fearless Mom community, as we believe in her vision of helping meet both spiritual AND physical needs around the world. I'm thrilled that this book will help others to understand and embrace this approach to living out our faith each and every day.

Julie Richard
Founder of Fearless Mom

Brace yourself, not only for an exhilarating exploration that stirs your soul but also allows you to ponder life a little deeper, igniting a desire to take meaningful action. Through her incredible experiences working with diverse individuals from around the world, Noel emerges as an extraordinary living example of selfless giving, boundless love, and the unwavering commitment to share help and hope with those in need. Her journey serves as a shining beacon, inspiring us all to step beyond the confines of our comfort zones and make a difference in the lives of others. As you immerse yourself in the vibrant tapestry of her words, you'll be encouraged to embrace the needs of others with open arms, to reflect upon your own abilities to make a difference for the Kingdom.

Sarah Nuse
Founder and CEO of Tippi Toes, author of *Destined for Greatness*

My oldest daughter Noel was only twelve years old when I decided to take her on her first missions trip. I was recovering from my first of eighteen surgeries. The doctors told me I had cancer, and I might not survive. I wanted Noel to see the way the rest of the world lived and to see it from God's perspective. Fast forward to today—not only did I survive cancer, but I was also able to take Noel on many more trips around the world. Today, she leads World Help, the organization I founded more than thirty years ago. Noel has a heart of compassion for the most vulnerable people and some of the most remote places. And I could not be prouder.

Vernon Brewer
Founder, World Help

BOTH

Noel Brewer Yeatts

**LIVING OUTSIDE THE
EITHER/OR OF YOUR FAITH**

Cover design by Joanna Person, www.joannagarciaart.com
Interior layout by Sean Smith, RSGCreate.com
Edited by Sheryl Martin Hash

Library of Congress Cataloging-in-Publication Data
Brewer Yeatts, Noel, 1972-
Both: Living outside the either/or of your faith / Noel Brewer Yeatts.
pages cm
Includes bibliographical references
ISBN 978-0-578-29734-7 (pbk.)
eBook ISBN 978-0-9788041-7-6
Audiobook ISBN 978-8-9887682-0-3
LCCN: 2023913421

All dates, place names, titles, and events in this account are factual. The names of some individuals have been changed in order to protect their privacy. Statistics used in this book were current at the time of publication.

For Pat, Riley, and Bentley.

I always take you with me.

III XI III XI

CONTENTS

INTRO

JESUS IN DISGUISE

> In a divided culture, Christians should
> be the help and the hope, not the hate.
> ~ Carey Nieuwhof[1]

A few years back, an Episcopal church in Davidson, North Carolina, became home to a very controversial statue. The sculpture is of a shrouded, obviously homeless man lying on a park bench by the church. The face and hands are obscured, but when you look closer, you see the nail-pierced feet of the man lying on the bench . . . and you realize it's Jesus.

Needless to say, the statue caused quite a stir in this wealthy community. Some church members, viewing it from a distance, thought the statue was human and reported the "homeless man" to the police, complaining of the nuisance and asking for him to be removed.

"That's right. Somebody called the cops on Jesus," a news article quipped.[2]

---

1 Carey Nieuwhof, "The Coming Church Split (It's Not What You Think)," CareyNieuwhof.com, August 21, 2022, https://careynieuwhof.com/the-coming-church-split-its-not-what-you-think/

2 John Burnett, "Statue of a Homeless Jesus Startles a Wealthy Community," NPR, April 13, 2014, https://www.npr.org/2014/04/13/302019921/statue-of-a-homeless-jesus-startles-a-wealthy-community

Others claimed that it was undignified to portray the Son of God as a hobo, saying that it demeans the church and the neighborhood. One man even said it was "creepy."

But I love the words of the minister of the church: "We believe that that's the kind of life Jesus had. He was, in essence, a homeless person. This is a relatively affluent church, to be honest, and we need to be reminded ourselves that our faith expresses itself in active concern for the marginalized of society."[3]

Mother Teresa once said, "When a poor person dies of hunger, it has not happened because God did not take care of him or her. It has happened because neither you nor I wanted to give that person what he or she needed."[4] In the poor we meet Jesus, she explained, in his most distressing disguises.

Jesus in disguise.

Christ reminds us of this when He addresses His disciples in the book of Matthew: "As you did it to one of the least of my brothers, you did it to me."[5]

Extending a helping hand in someone's darkest hour is the gospel in its introductory form. It is a sign—a landmark, a lighthouse pointing to the shore . . . pointing to hope.

It's a warm meal given in love to a refugee.
A cup of clean water for a thirsty child.
A lifesaving vaccine for a sick baby.

3 John Burnett, "Statue of a Homeless Jesus Startles a Wealthy Community," NPR, April 13, 2014, https://www.npr.org/2014/04/13/302019921/statue-of-a-homeless-jesus-startles-a-wealthy-community

4 "A Quote by Mother Teresa," Goodreads, accessed June 14, 2023, https://www.goodreads.com/quotes/405714-when-a-poor-person-dies-of-hunger-it-has-not

5 Matthew 25:40 (ESV)

Food and shelter for a refugee fleeing war.
A set of clean clothes for a homeless man.

Yet, instead of embracing this robust, holistic vision of how our faith is best expressed, we tend to make it an either/or choice—a carefully curated brand of the kind of Christian we are with little room to grow or expand.

It shouldn't come as a surprise. From our earliest experienes in life we are asked to see the world in black and white, to choose—a favorite color, food, music, song, place to travel, and the list goes on.

As we get older, the choices become more complicated—political party, church affiliation, denomination, kids' schools, friend groups, exercise routines, hobbies. You get the point.

Honestly, when I am asked to name my favorite anything I immediately tense up. It's just too much pressure. One thing? I have to name just one? I have learned that I am not a "favorite" kind of person. Maybe it is my people-pleasing personality, or maybe it is just that I love too many things.

Colors? Well, I really am partial to neutrals like black, white, and gray, but I love a good pop of color like yellow or green. And places to travel? How much time do you have? Church denominations? I have been a part of them all. Political party? Depends on the year. Music? Depends on the mood. Food? This one, I can tell you most definitely what I *don't* like: seafood.

Somebody can analyze later what this really says about me. Maybe I don't have favorites. Or maybe, I am afraid to choose.

Regardless, few of these choices, if any, are right and wrong or black and white. The truth is, most of life is lived in the gray. And too often we limit ourselves by living in the either/or when we could be living in the beauty and fullness of both. There's no way to be a perfect parent, or spouse, or Christian. But there are a million ways to be a faithful one.

Our world is so full of brokenness. Our communities can be so divisive. We sometimes only see what we are looking for. What if instead of looking for problems, conflict, brokenness, disease, and hunger, we opened our eyes and looked for signs of life?

What if we changed the conversation from what we can't do, to what we can? From those we can't help, to those we can. From guilt and charity to action, justice, and radical generosity.

What if we really could live beyond the either/or of our faith? A life that takes the gospel message so seriously that we care about the body and the soul, the physical and the spiritual. A faith so alive that we care about BOTH.

I believe Jesus is our best example of how to live this kind of life. In the words of author and pastor Louie Giglio:

> *Both things collide in the person of Jesus. Jesus is evangelism embodied. He's God in human flesh. That's evangelism at its core. It's heaven sending mercy and hope to earth. So Jesus was all about evangelism. That was his final mission: to give his life as a sacrifice for the sins of the world. That was his driving purpose. So you can't say, 'Well Jesus was just a philosopher or a teacher or a healer.' No, Jesus was an evangelist. . . . He was always locked on the mission of the cross. But on the way to the cross he healed*

the blind, he touched the lepers, he embraced prostitutes, he gave dignity to women and other marginalized people, he spoke out against injustice. He did some of those things to show he was the Messiah. But he did all of those things because God has a heart of compassion for people. The more we talk about Jesus, the more we see both of those things co-existing happily.[6]

The following pages will take you on a journey that gives you a glimpse into this kind of life—all it could be, and all it could change.

Together we will learn how to identify the pitfalls of disembodied faith throughout history and in our own lives. What it means to live out our faith according to Jesus's radical new kingdom rules. How valuing the needs of a whole person—body and soul—is holy, just, and transformational. And how embracing a life of "both" can meet the needs of people around the world and revitalize our own faith.

Living an integrated life of faith—one that embraces the sacred value and messy humanity of others near and far—is the next revolutionary chapter of "missions" as we know it. It's how we change the world for Christ. It's how we, ourselves, are changed.

Join me as we discover the power of BOTH.

---

6 Drew Dyck, "Louie Giglio: Passion for a Generation-Part 2," outreachmagazine.com, April 22, 2016, https://outreachmagazine.com/interviews/16583-louie-giglio-passion-for-a-generation-part-2.html

CHAPTER ONE / BEGINNING WITH BOTH IN MIND

THE BITTER AND THE SWEET

The aroma of Guatemalan coffee began to wake me up as I looked down on the hazy valley below. This was a place I had come to love; not just for the beauty, but for the people, the food, the culture, and the work—the beautiful, messy, heartbreaking work.

The air was still a bit cool and damp, as if it were trying to distract me from what was to come. But I knew better. Soon the temperatures would rise with a vengeance, and the air would become thick and unforgiving, dripping with humidity. But for now, it was just perfect. And I soaked up every single, fleeting second.

But as much as I enjoyed this Central American country, it was also a place that had taught me hard lessons about that thin line between life and death. How the lack of food and clean water affects even the tiniest of lives.

On one of my many visits, I met a little boy named Lex, who had been buried alive just days after his birth and saved by a neighbor. I attended the funeral of a baby boy we had tried to help just the day before. He fell ill during the night and died on the way to the hospital. Seeing his mother standing over his small casket was more than I could take—too much pain and sorrow to absorb in the space of a moment—and something I will never forget.

I held a little boy whose skin was about to burst with the fluid building up in his body. Local doctors informed the family he

... poverty robs people of choices.

had cancer and would not make it. We did not want to give up on this child and were determined to get him help. But days later, he passed away. I could tell you the stories of so many others— Diego, Margarite, Jose. For some, our help arrived too late. But for others, we were just in time.

More than any other place I have traveled, Guatemala is where I learned about the lives of those living in extreme poverty and how that poverty robs people of choices. And how, if left uninterrupted, it would become a vicious cycle that continues on for generations.

Despite all the things I loved about Guatemala, my heart could not ignore its dark side: how the lives of so many were cut short, just because they lacked access to basic resources. This place—the contagious joy and the overwhelming sorrow of it— had profoundly affected me.

THE END OF MISSIONS

I was 12 when I started traveling internationally with my dad; I thought I knew what "missions" was all about. I was full of passion. I was getting to serve people in ways that would shape me forever. But I didn't truly comprehend the magnitude of what drew me to this work. I had a stereotypical understanding of the word "missions"—one that limited the scope of its intended effect. And for years, I continued to approach my work in the same well-intended but stunted way.

Years later, I found myself in Guatemala that summer morning, drinking coffee at the top of a hill overlooking the breathtaking scenery and reflecting on my life's work. What did it all really mean? I had never felt "called" to traditional missions like so many before me. I never thought God wanted me to be a full-time missionary. And yet here I was—twenty plus years in—doing what I thought was "missions" work. I was confused and restless.

I realized at that moment how tired I was of the word "missions." How it had come to communicate something to which I could no longer relate. I couldn't find what I felt so strongly about within the space of that one little word—*missions.* After hearing it so many times, it had become another Christian catchphrase that cheapened the work I believed in by reducing it to a label and a choice.

As one by one these realizations hit, my mind started spinning. I could almost feel the old, worn-out parts of my heart begin to stir. A new passion started bubbling up inside me. One that wanted to disrupt things a bit, to change the way things have been done for hundreds of years, to breathe new life into this work, and to boldly join a new kind of people on a new kind of mission.

As I sat there wrestling through some of these feelings, the following words poured out, and I typed them as fast as I could on my phone:

I'm on a mission to end missions.

You see I don't like that word 'missions,' and I haven't for some time. I don't like it because it separates this work that we do from our 'real' lives. By defining it, we make it a choice. Something we can choose to do or not do, a project we can choose to get involved in or not. A trip we can choose to go on or not go on.

... it's all the same life—the good, the beautiful, and the ugly; the ups and downs; the highs and lows; the happy and the heartbreaking, the interesting and the seriously disturbing. And God can be found in all of it.

I used to think I had to separate everything . . . keep my personal and fun life separate from my 'mission work.' Now I know that what's more authentic is embracing it all—the good and beautiful and the hard and ugly—all at the same time.

So that means one minute I'm posting an article on how women and young girls around the world are being forced into the sex trade, and the next post is happy faces with my kids on a ball field. What I've learned is that it's all the same life—the good, the beautiful, and the ugly; the ups and downs; the highs and lows; the happy and the heartbreaking, the interesting and the seriously disturbing. And God can be found in all of it. He is not absent.

I'm not saying I completely understand why God allows suffering, and I won't try to justify it with cliché answers. The truth is I'm not sure I will ever fully understand suffering, pain, and poverty; and most days, I simply can't stand it.

And while I want to scream over senseless shootings and murders and break down crying when I see children suffer because they have no food or water, I hold on to the only truth I know: that a day is coming when the world is made new, and I long for that new world.

But until then, my calling, your calling, and the calling of all who claim to follow Jesus Christ, should be to restore hope. No judging, just love. No handouts, but a hand out of poverty. No guilt, but true compassion that comes only from meeting people right where they are.

This is what it truly means to live out our faith.

It's not called missions—it's called life.

I wrote those words more than six years ago, and yet, I feel them even more strongly today. Perhaps I would have spent a little more time to flesh them out and perfect the wording if I knew they were going to end up in a book. But, in essence, this is still what I believe and serves as the foundation of this book.

> It's not called
> missions—it's
> called life.

But ending missions? Really? As the leader of a global "missions" organization, that might create a few problems. So, let me explain.

WHAT IF?

First of all, let me be clear. I come from a long line of missions and ministry. Traditional missions has always been a part of my life, and I have a deep respect for the work that generations of missionaries have done to spread the hope of the gospel around the world. If it were not for them, I wouldn't be where I am or doing what I am doing today.

That being said, I do long for a *reimagining* of missions. I long for a reclamation of what's helpful and right and good, and a casting off of all the ways it has been co-opted or mismanaged. It is love—not disdain, or cynicism, or disrespect—behind my questions and criticisms. I believe if you truly love something, you long to see it healed. You long to see it whole and flourishing. I long to see missions transformed in a way that not only changes us, but changes the world.

> I believe if you truly love something, you long to see it healed.

Deconstruction has become such a trendy buzzword in recent years, especially when talking about faith. It seems as if everyone is "deconstructing" their faith these days, especially high-profile religious celebrities. And it seems like most deconstruction stories do not have happy endings.

But not all deconstruction is bad. Reevaluating our faith can be a good and healthy thing. Asking questions, challenging the status quo, and building a faith of our own can be beneficial. It can even, in the end, strengthen our faith. I believe deconstructing "missions" does not have to be a bad thing either.

The dictionary defines a missionary as:

- someone who attempts to convert others to a particular doctrine or program

- someone sent on a mission—especially a religious or charitable mission to a foreign country

- one who is to witness across cultures[1]

This, to me, is the traditional meaning of those words. But in the context of our faith and the original intent of Jesus, what should the definitions be?

What if missions is really more about truly loving our neighbors? What if it is more about teaching people how to live on earth, not just how to get to heaven? What if we didn't have to choose between the physical and spiritual when meeting people's needs? What if we didn't have to choose between social justice and salvation? What if it could really be about *both*?

> ## What if missions is really more about truly loving our neighbors?

It's said that in order to change things and envision the future you desire, you have to start with the end in mind.[2] So, if we want the earth to look a little more like heaven, how will that change the way we live today? How will it change the way we do "missions" today?

Even though I have my own issues with the word, I don't want the way we do missions to be the punch line of a joke. I don't

---

1 Vocabulary.com, s.v. "Missionary," accessed February 13, 2023, https://www.vocabulary.com/dictionary/missionary

2 "Habit-2." FranklinCovey, December 28, 2022. https://www.franklincovey.com/habit-2/

want it to be a badge of honor or a check in the box of what good Christians do. I don't want it to be an internship of sorts to complete in order to be a "good Christian."

I want it to be a *way of life*—a way of life for a person of faith. The colors that paint a picture of what we believe for the world to see. We go to the ends of the earth not because we believe we are the heroes and not because God needs us to accomplish His work, but because it is an expression of the faith we say we take so seriously.

> We go to the ends of the earth not because we believe we are the heroes and not because God needs us to accomplish His work, but because it is an expression of the faith we say we take so seriously.

It reminds me of what best-selling author Bob Goff said: "There's nothing wrong with matching shirts and wristbands. We just don't need them anymore . . . We don't need to go on 'missions trips' any longer. Jesus's friends never called them this. They knew love already had a name." [3]

The truth is, Jesus never went on a mission trip, did He? But the way He loved and lived His life was something the world had never seen. Everywhere He went, lives were changed, people were healed, and hope was restored.

3 Bob Goff, Everybody, Always, page 55.

When we forget about "missions" and call this what it really is—living out our faith—I believe a new, freeing world opens up to us. One that allows us to look at things differently, evaluate things differently, and live differently.

As a result of this small shift, we will see "mission trips" as simply an *exercise* of our faith, not the culmination. Our imaginations will expand beyond a single "missions emphasis week" at church and spill over into every day of the week, wherever we are. We won't have to wait for

> We will seek justice and healing and restoration of the world because, as children of God, we ourselves have been justified, healed, and restored.

the custom T-shirt to give us permission to go and make disciples. We won't be satisfied with part-time faithfulness or waiting around for God to clean up the world. We will seek justice and healing and restoration of the world because, as children of God, we ourselves have been justified, healed, and restored. Instead of occasional volunteers, we will see ourselves as whole participants in the kingdom work of making the world new.

Missions is how we *live*. It should consume us in our homes, across the street, in our churches, in our places of work, and yes, in places of injustice around the world too. It should inspire us to seek human flourishing, to make wrong things right, and to bring the kingdom of God to the home we all share.

That is the story of World Help and the story behind our anchoring belief in "help and hope." You see, we believe that without food, access to clean water, and medicines that the body needs, the faith we profess means very little. But without faith that feeds the soul, meeting those physical needs is just a short-term fix. It's when you focus on both *body and soul* that true transformation happens in someone's life. It's when you meet the urgent physical and spiritual needs of today that hope has the space to dream of a better tomorrow.

And while some may refer to our work simply as "missions," I challenge them to broaden their thinking and to open their eyes to what God intends for us to do and be. To see that changing the world comes not from how much we are involved in "missions" but from lives filled with love. This love is living and expansive. It naturally spills out from our homes to our neighborhoods, our communities, and around the world. A love that compels us to respond to the needs of our world with both help and hope.

Both. Never either/or. Never one or the other. It is the combination of meeting people's physical and spiritual needs that gives help for today and hope for tomorrow to people in need. *Both* is the secret that empowers us to live out our faith and truly change the world.

 Scan the QR code for photos, videos, and more details about the stories from around the world shared in this chapter.

CHAPTER
TWO
CHASING AFTER
EITHER/OR

SANITIZED FAITH

A few years ago, I boarded a flight with a colleague and made my way to my seat. I noticed my coworker immediately proceeded to sanitize everything around him. This was pre-COVID. I have to say, he was ahead of his time.

With the methodical approach of a criminal trying to cover his tracks at a crime scene, he wiped his seat, then opened the tray table and wiped it down, too. He wiped down the armrests, and because he had a window seat, he even wiped down *the entire wall*. I'm sure it was the cleanest airplane seat that had ever been (or ever would be). I watched him in disbelief and mild amusement. His dedication to the cause was something to behold.

Finally, he appeared satisfied with his work and was about to sit down . . . when he realized he was in *the wrong row*. His seat was actually a row back. And again, everyone around watched curiously as he repeated the whole tedious ritual.

Telling that story used to be funny, but post-pandemic, there's a certain tinge of irony to it. Most of us wouldn't bat an eyelash if we saw someone doing this today.

The point is, we all can relate to the desperate need to protect ourselves and to make ourselves feel safe and clean. And hand sanitizers, in whatever form, are a small measure to help us do just that.

But what we don't like to admit or acknowledge about sanitizer is that some research shows it can actually lower your immunity and make you even more susceptible to germs.

A *New York Times* article about the pros and cons of hand sanitizer said that if it doesn't contain a high enough percentage of alcohol, then it doesn't kill any bacteria, and, "If anything . . . the gel seemed to mobilize the bacteria, spreading them around the hand instead of killing them."[1]

According to a World Health Organization report, our obsession with germ killing has resulted in antibiotic-resistant bacteria in every corner of the globe. Sanitizers, in fact, can leave residue. This residue continues to kill bacteria but not effectively, which allows stronger bacteria to survive and develop resistance.[2] So basically, hand sanitizer makes us *feel* clean, but the reality under a microscope might be totally different.

I started thinking about how this idea relates to our faith and the gospel. You see, while sanitizing our lives makes sense when fighting a virus, it doesn't make sense when applied to our faith.

---

1 Franklin, Deborah. "Hand Sanitizers, Good or Bad?" The New York Times. The New York Times, March 21, 2006. https://www.nytimes.com/2006/03/21/health/hand-sanitizers-good-or-bad.html.

2 Bill Saporito, "Why You Should Stop Using Hand Sanitizer," Time, May 12, 2014, https://time.com/96112/why-im-breaking-up-with-hand-sanitizer/.

Let me explain. A few years ago, I came home from a trip to Southeast Asia a bit stunned. I had found myself on the front lines of human trafficking—and I was not prepared for what I experienced. It was dark. It was dirty. It was vulgar. It was dehumanizing. It was degrading. It was overwhelming. At times, I felt hopeless.

My first Sunday back at my home church was a blur except for one part of the sermon. I remember my pastor saying, "God is with us in the dark places." And at that moment, I thought, *No, I'm not so sure about that.* I had just experienced some pretty dark places, and even though I looked, I couldn't find God there. I wanted to desperately, but it all just felt too filthy and wicked for God.

> **I had wiped away any trace of God's presence because I couldn't tolerate the backdrop.**

I struggled to process this overwhelming feeling for months before the realization crashed down on me like a ton of bricks: *It was me. I was the one who made God disappear.* God was not absent; I had just decided He did not fit there. I had decided He did not belong there in all that darkness and despair. Just like someone who is desperate to feel clean and safe from a deadly disease, I had reached for my sanitizer. But what I had sanitized instead was the gospel. I had wiped away any trace of God's presence because I couldn't tolerate the backdrop. What I ended up with felt clean, but it was hollow—it lacked substance. Not at all like good news. Not at all like the gospel.

A CASTLE, A CONGREGATION, AND A COVER-UP

Cape Coast Castle is located in central Ghana. This castle was originally used for trading and then as a fort. But during the height of the transatlantic slave trade, it was primarily used to house captives while they awaited transport to the New World.[3]

Dungeons beneath the structure held up to 1,500 slaves at one time for as long as three months. Hundreds were crammed into tiny rooms. They were chained and forced to lie in their own urine and feces for months.[4] Can you imagine the smells and the absolutely horrific conditions?

Today, Cape Coast Castle is a tourist attraction. I heard a conference speaker share about taking a tour there. Her tour guide led the group through the dungeons, and as they stood in those rooms where so many were once chained, he told them something unthinkable. He said, "Guess what is right above these dungeons? A chapel!"[5]

> And all the while there was unspeakable suffering right beneath them.

Think about that. A chapel. A place of worship right above those horrible dungeons. So, while hundreds were held captive, people in the chapel above probably sang, prayed, read Scripture,

3 "Cape Coast Castle." Wikipedia. Wikimedia Foundation, February 5, 2023. https://en.wikipedia.org/wiki/Cape_Coast_Castle.

4 Ugc. "A Former 'Slave Castle' on Africa's Gold Coast Still Stands." Atlas Obscura. Atlas Obscura, June 29, 2016. https://www.atlasobscura.com/places/cape-coast-castle

5 ""Trauma as a Place of Service—Q Talk." YouTube. YouTube, March 20, 2020 https://www.youtube.com/watch?app=desktop&v=YpDGzHb5DnQ.

and perhaps even took an offering for the less fortunate. And all the while there was unspeakable suffering right beneath them.

Then the guide said, "Heaven was above but hell was below."[6]

Fast forward to World War II Germany.

In his book, *When a Nation Forgets God*, Erwin Lutzer shares this powerful eyewitness account of a Christian who lived in Germany during the Nazi Holocaust:

> *We had heard stories of what was happening to the Jews, but we tried to distance ourselves from it, because, what could anyone do to stop it? A railroad track ran behind our small church and each Sunday morning we could hear the whistle in the distance and then the wheels coming over the tracks. We became disturbed when we heard the cries coming from the train as it passed by. We realized it was carrying Jews like cattle in cars!*
>
> *Week after week the whistle would blow. We dreaded to hear the sounds of those wheels because we knew that we would hear the cries of the Jews en route to a death camp. Their screams tormented us.*
>
> *We knew exactly at what time that whistle would blow, and we decided the only way to keep from being so disturbed by the cries was to start singing our hymns. By the time that train came rumbling past the church yard, we were singing at the top of our voices. If some of the screams reached our ears, we'd just sing a little louder until we could hear them no more.*

6 "Trauma as a Place of Service—Q Talk." YouTube. YouTube, March 20, 2020.
   https://www.youtube.com/watch?app=desktop&v=YpDGzHb5DnQ.

*Years have passed and no one talks about it anymore. But I
still hear the train whistle in my sleep. God forgive me; forgive all of us who called ourselves Christians yet did nothing
to intervene.*[7]

They just sang louder.

Fast forward to recent years where more and more victims of
sexual abuse in the church have come forward. The crisis spans
denominations and all levels of leadership, affecting thousands
of people over the past few decades alone. What we are seeing
now is a mass reckoning.

In his scathing article, Russell Moore, the former head of the
Southern Baptist Convention's Ethics and Religious Liberty
Commission, called the sexual abuse scandal of the SBC, "the
Southern Baptist apocalypse." He went on to say:

*Who cannot now see the rot in a culture that mobilizes to
exile churches that call a woman on staff a 'pastor' or that
invite a woman to speak from the pulpit on Mother's Day,
but dismisses rape and molestation as 'distractions' and efforts
to address them as violations of cherished church autonomy?
In sectors of today's SBC, women wearing leggings is a social
media crisis; dealing with rape in the church is a distraction.*

*I only know firsthand the rage of one who wonders while
reading what happened on the seventh floor of that Southern Baptist building, how many children were raped, how
many people were assaulted, how many screams were silenced,*

7 "Lutzer, Erwin W. When a nation forgets God: 7 lessons we must learn from Nazi Germany. Moody Publishers, 2015.

while we boasted that no one could reach the world for Jesus like we could. That's more than a crisis. It's even more than just a crime. It's blasphemy. And anyone who cares about heaven ought to be mad as hell.[8]

What do these three stories have in common? What do the dungeons of the transatlantic slave era, the cattle cars of Nazi concentration camps, and the hidden corners of churches across our own nation have in common?

For one, they were locations where unspeakable evil took place; second, they were all happening in the direct vicinity of worship, prayer, and large gatherings of Christians. I believe these incidents would not have happened without a deliberate sanitizing of the gospel.

> ... the lived experiences of human beings made in God's image have been utterly neglected, ignored, or worst of all, quietly tolerated.

I believe we have sanitized our faith to the point that the real, everyday problems and physical needs—the lived experiences of human beings made in God's image—have been utterly neglected, ignored, or worst of all, quietly tolerated.

And just like that former dungeon on the Ghanaian coast, there are still many dungeons here on earth. Dungeons of poverty, dungeons of disease, dungeons of slavery, abuse, fear, and hopelessness.

8 Moore, Russell. "This Is the Southern Baptist Apocalypse." ChristianityToday.com. Christianity Today, May 22, 2022. https://www.christianitytoday.com/ct/2022/may-web-only/southern-baptist-abuse-apocalypse-russell-moore.html

As people of faith, we cannot remain numb and blind to the suffering around us. No, we need to go into the dungeons—reach right into the dungeons of this world, embrace the dungeons of the world, charge into the dungeons of the world—until the dungeons look a little more like heaven. That is what our lives should be all about.

THE COST OF SEPARATING BODY AND SOUL

Sometimes people question my work and the ethos of World Help. People who don't associate themselves with a particular faith may say, "Why do you focus so much on spiritual development?" At the same time, most Christ-followers would ask the opposite: "Why the humanitarian aid? It's only a temporary fix for a spiritual problem."

They are both valid questions. What is more important—meeting physical needs for today or feeding the soul? But they are questions that only make sense if you actually believe you can separate the two. We have been conditioned to believe in this false dichotomy, and if you grew up in church, you probably received a double dose.

Our culture teaches us that the only way to succeed is to be a workaholic—to be a machine, always producing. It's only in recent years that the ideas of rest, mental health, and work-life balance have gained popularity and traction.

Growing up in church, I heard the numbers of attendance and salvation. In some churches there were (and still are) literal signs on the wall with the numbers on them like the scoreboard at a basketball game. For some time, these were the only metrics used to measure how a church or ministry was doing.

And in "missions" it was true as well. We learned to obsess over counting how many hands were raised during the sinner's prayer or how many people rededicated their lives to Christ. These precious professions of faith became a sort of currency, like little badges of honor to prove the success of the church's work on "the mission field."

I vividly remember my first "missions" trip to Korea as a child. I was with my dad and a group of college students. On the bus, I sat watching an older couple with us intentionally toss tracts out the windows to people on the street.

If you don't know what a tract is, it is basically a small evangelistic booklet or pamphlet. They are not as common today, but they were a staple of a "good Christian" when I was growing up.

A friend shared how when she was in college, she worked as a server at Olive Garden. She said the after-church lunch crowd on Sundays was by far the worst shift to work. The people were characteristically grumpy, rude, and impatient. None of the servers wanted that shift and would always trade with the new team members who didn't know better. And to add insult to injury, let's just say these church people were not the best tippers. She told me how many of them left a tract that looked like a dollar bill, instead of a real tip.

Now, don't get me wrong. I am not making fun of the use of tracts. There are countless people who have found God through literature like this. In fact, even today in some persecuted countries where people face death for sharing their faith, "gospel balloons" filled with literature are sent to share the love of Christ with the otherwise unreachable. What I am saying is that when we do have the opportunity to reach people in a personal way—but opt instead to throw our "message of hope" out the window—it gives the appearance of only caring about a person's final destination and not actually caring about, well, *them*.

Did the tracts thrown out the bus window or left in a restaurant booth help anyone? Probably. Could that work have been more strategic? Absolutely yes. And could it have been done in a way that also showed we cared about their lives, their struggles, their hopes, and dreams? Yes. It could have accomplished both.

There is nothing wrong with good, old-fashioned "soul winning." But there is a danger in this as well. When we elevate soul counts over people, we fall back into bad habits that have been around for thousands of years.

THE ROOTS OF EITHER/OR FAITH

The idea that the physical body is separate and inferior to the eternal soul can be traced back to the first few centuries after Christ.

Heresies like Gnosticism and Docetism taught that the body was the source of all evil, too lowly to be welcomed into the eternal kingdom of God. They denied the reality of the incarnation and claimed that though Jesus appeared to be a real human, He didn't have actual flesh and bones.

Why was this idea so devastating?

Well, if you can deny that Jesus chose to assume a human body, engage in the physical human experience, and suffer a human death, why should the bodies of other people made in His image matter to you? Why concern yourself with the experiences of the poor and the suffering of the sick? After all, if heaven is the only goal, what happens on earth is no longer your responsibility, right? If the body is the source of all suffering and evil, why bother comforting the afflicted or seeking justice for the oppressed?

One article sums it up like this:

> *Unfortunately, traces of Gnostic thought continue to permeate the thinking of many well-meaning Christians today. For example, some Christians think that only two things will last into eternity: God's Word and the souls of men and women—an emphasis on the spiritual and an exclusion of the physical. But this is wrong. The Bible explicitly teaches that not only will these two last into eternity but so will our bodies, in a glorified state (John 5:28-29; 1 Corinthians 15:42-44). . . . James warns us that 'pure and undefiled religion in the sight of our God and Father is this: to visit orphans and widows in their distress, and to keep oneself unstained by the world' (James 1:27). However, don't make the mistake that believing the converse is true either, that the body is more important than the spirit. Both have equal importance in the eyes of God.*[9]

9 Jeter, Derrick G. "Mind over Matter: The Heresy of Gnosticism Both Then and Now." Crosswalk.com. Crosswalk.com, February 8, 2010. https://www.crosswalk.com/faith/spiritual-life/mind-over-matter-the-heresy-of-gnosticism-both-then-and-now-11625938.html.

I love this quote because it shows that God cares about our bodies and bodily needs so much that when we die, we are given a new body in a "glorified state." And when Jesus rose from the dead, He appeared not as a spirit but in a real body. And while His body was incorruptible, think about this: In the days following Jesus's resurrection, what do we see Him doing? Not only do we find Him showing the scars on His very real body, but we also find Him eating. And why? Because that is what a real body needs to survive. And that is what people who are alive do. Our bodies are made in the very image of God, and they matter.

> Our bodies are made in the very image of God, and they matter.

When it comes down to it, if you reduce the point of life to either/or, all or nothing, body or soul, us or them, then you never have to wade into the messiness of both. You deny the gift of seeing the full image of God in a person. You begin to dehumanize those around you by reducing them to a soul to be saved or damned.

The truth is, the "both" we're talking about—the both that sees the needs of a whole person—is rarely certain, never safe, and hardly ever predictable. But we can almost always find the beauty in it if we are willing to look hard enough. In fact, it's in the messiness of both where we find God Himself.

"THIS IS NOT MY HOME"

It was the end of a long day, and I was completely overwhelmed. Every single one of our partners seemed to be in crisis. The pandemic had pushed people already living in extreme poverty to the brink, and food was, by far, the most crucial need. But it didn't stop there.

I watched in utter disbelief as the horrific events in Afghanistan unfolded on the screen in front of me. It was August 2021, and the United States had just announced plans to pull out of the country after decades of military presence. I'm sure you remember watching the crowds of people rush to the Kabul airport, fighting to get in, and literally climbing onto the wheels of moving planes to escape.

The human suffering was more than I could bear, and my only coherent thought was more of a plea: *Jesus, come quickly.*

> But you know, I think when we proclaim, "this isn't our home," it inadvertently says to the rest of the world, "the pain you are experiencing now isn't really my problem. After all, I have heaven to look forward to."

As they desperately try to make sense of humanitarian disasters like this, well-meaning people of faith often repeat a common refrain: "We need to remember this is not our home." In other words, the here and now is just a waiting room for eternity.

I know people have good intentions when they say this. I've probably said it myself. It's easy to say things like this when the human suffering we see can't be explained. It helps us remember where we are going, and that this earth is our temporary home.

But you know, I think when we proclaim, "this isn't our home," it inadvertently says to the rest of the world, "the pain you are experiencing now isn't really my problem. After all, I have heaven to look forward to."

The incarnation itself shows us that the here and now matters to God too. The nitty gritty experience of life in a human body matters so much that Jesus came to us in the form of a baby and lived 33 years in this world before he went "home" to the right hand of the Father. The kingdom of heaven isn't what we're waiting for; the kingdom of heaven is here. It is now.

In Matthew 3:2, John the Baptist, calling for repentance, says, "Change your life. God's kingdom is here." [10]

Author Gabe Lyons writes extensively about our calling as Christ's followers to restore:

> *Telling others about Jesus is important, but conversion isn't their only motive. Their mission is to infuse the world with beauty, grace, justice, and love. I call them restorers because they envision the world as it was meant to be, and they work toward that vision. Restorers seek to mend the earth's brokenness. They recognize that the world will not be completely healed until Christ's return, but they believe the process begins now as we partner with God. Through sowing seeds of restoration, they believe others will see Christ through us, and the Christian faith will reap a much larger harvest.* [11]

---

10 Matthew 3:2 (MSG)

11 Gabe Lyons, The Next Christians: The Good News About the End of Christian America, page 47.

You see, we are meant to be at work bringing heaven TO earth—not biding our time, waiting for something better. And while this may not be our forever home, *it is our home right now.* God is inviting us to restore all that has been broken. To build His kingdom right here on earth. To restore everything that sin has taken away.

Have you sanitized your faith to the point where it makes you feel safe in your world? What would it take to reclaim it in all its uncertainty—in all its messiness?

So often throughout the church's history, we have turned the gospel into something that only meets our needs and fits inside the safety of our churches and homes.

But it was meant for so much more. We were meant for so much more.

Scan the QR code for photos, videos, and more details about the stories from around the world shared in this chapter.

CHAPTER THREE

THE MEANING OF BOTH

HALLELUJAH

As I woke up that morning in Uganda, I expected it to be a day like any other—one where our team would follow a set schedule, one with a predictable ending.

We had landed right after the president announced a new COVID-19 lockdown for the next forty-two days. All citizens had to choose a district to stay in for the next six weeks, so our time and travel were limited.

I had been to this country a number of times, so I knew our itinerary for the day. We would visit several of our programs, see a new maternity clinic under construction, and distribute some bicycles. I knew it would be hot because, it turns out, most places I travel are, to put it mildly, absolutely sweltering.

But that was the only thing that went as expected. Although the memories of the heat being so intense and relentless that I felt as if I would melt are starting to fade, there are other memories from that day that I will never be able to shake.

We spent the morning with our Ugandan partner of more than twenty years. The length of that partnership means countless stories and countless lives changed. Years of listening—really listening—to what the true needs of this country are from the people who know best. Years of learning what our role is, and how we can come alongside and resource those who already know what to do and how to do it.

> **Most women here go through an entire pregnancy without seeing a doctor or receiving any kind of prenatal care.**

The maternity clinic was impressive. I walked through it as the construction crew continued to work around me. Then, all at once, the weight of the impact of this building hit me. Safe motherhood is a luxury in places like rural Uganda, and this clinic will give so many new moms the help they desperately need.

The clinic is strategically located more than twenty miles from the nearest district hospital and forty miles from the nearest major hospital. And in a place where transportation is not easily accessible, those miles can mean a journey of days, not minutes. The small health facilities within this district face inadequate medical staff and insufficient supplies of medications; most are not equipped to handle much more than simple first aid.

Most women here go through an entire pregnancy without seeing a doctor or receiving any kind of prenatal care. That means no assessment of the mother or baby and no education about nutrition or safe practices during pregnancy or delivery. Many Ugandans in remote areas still hold a belief in mysticism and will turn to natural remedies and witchcraft if they cannot obtain medical care.

So not only is this maternity clinic the first of its kind in the area, but it will also provide urgent physical care for the community while providing information to young women so they can better understand how to care for themselves.

Medical teams from the maternity clinic will visit the schools and villages to educate girls on the importance of self-respect, healthy living, and the dangers of sexually transmitted diseases. The facility will also offer services beyond maternal care, including lab work, HIV/AIDS consultations, support and treatment, immunizations, child-care training, and so much more.

The maternity clinic will provide care for approximately twenty expectant mothers per month and assist about 420 new mothers each year. Like I said, impressive.

As we ended the tour of the facility, a crowd gathered in the middle of the construction. It was a group of church planters that serves in this area of Uganda—only this was a unique group. They had formed a co-op of sorts to help and support each other in their work, sharing resources and training.

Most of them regularly walked across entire counties just to reach their church members, especially during the pandemic when worshipers could not meet in person. During their visits, the church planters not only encouraged people in their faith, but also delivered the food and supplies families needed to stay alive. With the new lockdown coming, this help would be needed more than ever.

Then I learned something astonishing: this dedicated group had been praying for *years* for bicycles to travel from home to home and town to town. I literally had to ask if I heard that right. Praying for years?

Our distribution that day wasn't commonplace or ordinary—it was an answer to hundreds of prayers. The gift of the bicycles meant the hope of Christ could be shared with hundreds more. It meant being able to deliver lifesaving supplies, to literally keep people alive.

One of the co-op leaders was reading from a list. The members had decided amongst themselves who needed these bikes the most. And, one by one, the names of the recipients were announced.

As I helped pull the bikes off the truck and hand them to the church planters, something incredible happened. One at a time, they broke out into a chorus of "Hallelujahs," raising their hands and praising God at the top of their lungs. Their excitement and passion were contagious.

One church planter shared, "We have been walking on foot. Now our work has been simplified, and it means God is at work. You boosted it. Even as the churches are closing down, we are going to use these bicycles to reach people, to go where they are in their home places. Thank you very much. You are spreading the gospel far from where you are now. God bless you."

I can't think of a better example of how meeting physical and spiritual needs ushers in help and hope. I'll never forget those joyful shouts of "hallelujah" as years of prayers were finally answered. And they will forever serve as a reminder that I, too, have so much for which to be thankful—so many hallelujahs to shout.

> **Sometimes hallelujah arrives on two wheels.**

Sometimes a bicycle is the best way to deliver help and help. And sometimes hallelujah arrives on two wheels.

GENIUS OF THE AND

In his groundbreaking book, *Built to Last,*[1] leadership researcher, expert, and author Jim Collins talks about an interesting concept. He discusses the "Tyranny of the OR" and the "Genius of the AND." He explains that the "Tyranny of the OR pushes people to believe that things must be either A or B, but not both."

But visionary companies free themselves of this thinking with the "Genius of the AND." They are able to hold two seemingly opposing concepts or goals at the same time. In the business world, this shows up in prioritizing things like purpose AND profit, analysis AND action, discipline AND creativity.[2]

Too many times over the years, I have heard the debate. Too many times, I have had to defend our work from the "Tyranny of the OR." Some people ask why we focus on only meeting peo-

---

1 Collins, James C. Built to Last, 3rd ed., HarperBusiness, 2002.

2 "Genius of the And," Jim Collins—Concepts—Genius of the AND. Accessed February 13, 2023. https://www.jimcollins.com/concepts/genius-of-the-and.html.

ple's spiritual needs. Don't we know they are dying from the lack of clean water? While others can't understand why we focus so much on "social justice" issues that appear not to have any effect on a person's soul.

Two seemingly opposing ideas or strategies. The "Tyranny of the OR."

But what if we embraced the "Genius of the AND"?

It makes me think of the time a Cuban church planter stood up to share his testimony in a room full of fellow church planters. This particular man caught my attention because he was wearing a familiar purple jacket and shirt that I recognized had come from one of World Help's aid shipments. We've had the privilege of supporting church-planting efforts in Cuba since 2010. That day, we listened to one courageous individual after another share stories of the everyday realities they faced in their work—hardship and danger, need and difficulty; but most of all, hope.

The man in the purple jacket told us how he felt a burden for a rural area of Cuba where there was no ministry work at all. Someone had donated a piece of land to him, and he had been able to build a small home where the locals could meet. Every Saturday, about sixty kids gathered at this new home. Through our partnership, the church planter was able to give each child a Bible—but he was also able to do so much more.

Seeing a collection of sports jerseys in one of our recent shipments, the church planter got an idea. Even though the shirts were sized for adults, he had them altered to fit the kids so they could form a soccer team with matching uniforms. You have to understand what a big deal this is. To form a soccer team in this part of Cuba AND to have new matching uniforms was unheard of.

News of the matching soccer jerseys spread to surrounding villages, attracting excited crowds of children who hoped to be part of the new team. And let's just say, the church is growing! As he continued to share with us, the church planter asked for just one thing: more Bibles to help continue his work.

I love this story because there is no greater example of how everything we do all works together. From the donated clothes and aid that we are able to ship, to the training of church planters, to the provision of Bibles—all of that together is what changes lives. **Help *and* Hope**.

As I write this, World Help is celebrating our thirty-year anniversary. And let me tell you, a lot has changed in those three decades.

- In the early '90s, we were still using dial-up internet, and the world wide web had just been made available to everyone
- *Dances with Wolves* won the Oscar for best picture that year
- Parachute pants were all the rage
- The Soviet Union was dissolved
- Michael Bolton topped the charts with "When a Man Loves a Woman"
- A VCR could set you back $399

- And if you were lucky enough to have a cell phone, it was probably the size of a small child

Thirty years ago, I was a college student working for my dad and helping stuff envelopes for this new organization he had just started. I stuffed *a lot* of envelopes in our little three-room office.

Our lives and the world have changed so much over the past thirty years.

In the very early days of World Help, 36 percent of the world survived on a dollar and ninety cents a day or less. Today it is down to 9 percent.[3]

Back then, 52 percent of the world's poorest people lived in East Asia and the Pacific. As of 2015, they represented only 6 percent.[4]

Approximately 35,000 children under the age of 5 died every day from preventable causes. We're talking hunger. Disease. Lack of clean water.

Today, that number has shrunk by more than half.[5]

And millions more people have access to God's Word through increased distribution and digital availability.

In the face of so many overwhelming issues today, it's easy to

---

3 "Schoch, Marta, Christoph Lakner, and Melina Fleury. "Progress toward Ending Poverty Has Slowed," World Bank Blogs, October 16, 2020. https://blogs.worldbank.org/opendata/progress-toward-ending-poverty-has-slowed.

4 "Poverty Trends: Global, Regional and National," Development Initiatives, December 2019. https://www.devinit.org/resources/poverty-trends-global-regional-and-national/

5 "Children: Improving Survival and Well-Being," World Health Organization. World Health Organization, September 8, 2022 https://www.who.int/news-room/fact-sheets/detail/children-reducing-mortality

think that nothing we can do makes a difference.

But that simply isn't true. The numbers have significantly improved. And the World Help family has been a part of that.

> In the face of so many overwhelming issues today, it's easy to think that nothing we can do makes a difference.

As I write this book, we have seen more than 80 million lives transformed through Bible distribution, church planting, clean water projects, lifesaving aid shipped and delivered to people in need, malnourished babies rescued and brought back to health, women set free from the sex industry, and so much more.

To me, that's not a reason to stop; it's motivation to keep going.

1-2 PUNCH

A few years ago, I decided I wanted to try boxing. I'm not sure I was really all in, but I just wanted to give it a try.

Now, I like to work out and do CrossFit-type things, but I am no athlete—never have been. I was a cheerleader growing up, but that was before cheerleading was considered a sport.

But I thought boxing could add a bit of variety to my normal routine. It's a great way to de-stress and let off some steam, and, if I learned to do it right, it could even be a great self-defense tool. Right now, I think I am actually more of a danger to myself!

So I started with a couple of lessons. I ordered the right equipment. Like most sports, having the correct gear is the first step, right? When I took up golf, I think I cared more about my golf clothes and my club headcovers than I did about my game. Tennis had me all sorts of distracted by all the cute skirts you can wear.

I still remember when I decided to play softball in middle school. My dad was so excited. He had all daughters at the time, so he was over the moon when one of us finally wanted to play a sport. We went out and bought a nice glove, and he spent hours breaking that glove in. Putting oil on, working it in. One of my first times out on the field, I broke my finger. (I still don't know how it happened!) With a bulky new finger splint, I couldn't get that perfect glove on anymore, and that was the end of my illustrious softball career—but at least I had a nice glove.

So, with this history in mind, it was no surprise that when I took up boxing, I had to buy bright pink boxing gloves. I mean, what screams tough more than pink boxing gloves? Well, it doesn't really matter because my interest didn't last long. But it lasted long enough for me to learn a thing or two.

I learned there are four basic moves in boxing: the jab, the cross, the hook, and the bob and weave. I know, with all this groundbreaking knowledge, I'm practically Rocky—but bear with me.

One of the first movements I practiced is commonly referred to as the "1-2 punch." It is a combination of two of the basic moves: the jab and the cross. More precisely, the "1-2 punch" is defined as "an especially forceful or effective combination or sequence of two things." It's the foundation for all other punches. If you don't get it right, nothing else really works.

The 1-2 punch is a move that's inseparable. You can't achieve the same result if you do one move or the other by itself. If you just learn the jab (punch 1), your opponent knows what to expect.

Punch 2, the cross, is where all your power comes from. The combination is what makes the move so effective. If you don't learn the 1-2, you won't be competitive. All of boxing is based on this fundamental move.

Think about it. The phrase "1-2 punch" has become part of our everyday vocabulary. We use it to explain when two things—good or bad—happen together.

I can't help but relate the "1-2 punch" to the mission of World Help—help for today and hope for tomorrow. Together, these "punches" change the world.

It reminds me of the day a special guest showed up at our offices.

Gary Habermas is an American historian, New Testament scholar, and philosopher of religion. He is most famous for his 1985 debate on the resurrection against then world-famous atheist Antony Flew. Gary was featured in the film *The Case for Christ*, and he also happens to be a friend of my dad's.

As the story goes, when my dad was battling cancer and had just had surgery to remove a tumor, he could not speak because he had a tube down his throat. It was the night before Gary's famous debate with Flew, and yet, he still found time to come and visit my dad in the hospital.

Since my dad couldn't talk, my mom handed him a clipboard, and he scribbled on a piece of paper, "Beat Flew." Gary and my dad still reminisce about that moment every time they see each other. Now, years later, Gary was here to share with our team, and I couldn't wait to soak up every word. He started with a well-known passage found in Matthew:

"'Love the Lord your God with all your heart and with all your soul and with all your mind.' This is the first and greatest commandment. And the second is like it: 'Love your neighbor as yourself.'"[6]

Now if you grew up in church, you are most likely familiar with these verses, right? We are taught from a very young age that the most important part of being a Christian is to love God and love others. But Gary Habermas told it in a fresh way. He pointed out that these commands are numbered. And they are numbered in a way found nowhere else in Scripture.

1: Love God

2: Love your neighbor

He told us that Jesus numbers "Loving God" as number 1 and "loving your neighbor" as number 2—the first and second greatest commandments! He said that nowhere else in the gospel do we hear a numerical list like this. But here we see number 1 and number 2. These are God's top two priorities.

6 Matthew 22:37-38 (NIV)

He explained that these instructions were higher in importance than all the things we frequently debate as Christians. Even for Gary, a world-renowned debater, loving our neighbor was far more important than being "right," even on important matters.

He went on to talk about all the politics and bickering we see on social media or even in our own churches. And sadly, as we are debating all of these other things, these two commands often fall by the wayside.

Personally, I think it is easier for us to accept number 1, to say that loving God is most important. But loving your neighbor—what Jesus calls "number 2"—is crucial. The second greatest thing we can do after loving God is to love those around us.

How we go about doing number 1—loving God—is *directly related* to how we practice number 2, loving our neighbors. I would almost go so far as to say that you can't do one without the other.

> **The second greatest thing we can do after loving God is to love those around us.**

I think it's easy for us to get comfortable with number 1. We love God. We go to church. We read our Bibles, and we truly feel good about that. But is that the whole picture? The Bible also says the world will know we truly belong to God by how well we love each other.[7]

Let's be honest. Loving our neighbors can feel scary, sacrificial, and uncomfortable. But isn't that exactly how we are meant to live?

7 John 13:35 (NIV)

I believe the truest expression of our love for God is reflected in how well we love others. It is the manifestation of our faith. In order to love others well, we must love God well. And once we love God with everything, we will be driven to love others. We will be compelled to charge into the darkness with the love and hope of Christ. We will be burdened for what burdens the heart of God.

Loving God AND loving people.

Loving people—not in spite of, but *because*—because of our love for God.

A 1-2 punch.

Lives are changed when we first love God with all our heart.

The natural outcome of that love toward God is an outpouring of love for our neighbors. You can't have one without the other. We can't follow Christ without loving the people He made in His image.

KNOCKING OUT THE NEEDS OF THE WORLD

I was with my dad the first time I visited Cancer Hospital #62 just outside of Moscow. It was a hard visit. Dad had survived cancer only a few years earlier, and the visit brought back painful memories. A cancer hospital was the last place he wanted to be.

It was the leading cancer hospital in Russia at the time. But even the top doctors could not make up for the lack of resources, medicine, and supplies. People were sent here to die.

The hospital was surviving on almost nothing. The medicine cabinets were empty, there were no bandages for wounds, and plastic straws were being used for tracheotomies. In fact, each night, two people washed rubber latex gloves so they could be reused the next day. (Yes, that's what I said—*reused*!)

The chief surgeon was a man named Dr. Mahkson. He asked us for help, and my dad promised him we would send it as soon as possible—and we did. We were able to ship thirteen ocean-going containers full of supplies valued at over $2 million!

That was the beginning of our humanitarian aid work at World Help. Thanks to individual supporters, businesses, doctor's offices, companies, hospitals, and grants, hundreds of millions of dollars' worth of vital medical supplies, equipment, food, and other aid have been shipped and distributed around the world impacting millions of people . . . and it continues to grow.

> We can't follow Christ without loving the people He made in His image.

But back to the cancer hospital. I was there the week that one of these containers was delivered. I saw doctors literally running out of surgery, ripping open the boxes, and pulling out tubing or some piece of equipment they needed for surgery right at that moment. It was incredible.

Dr. Mahkson came up to me and said, "Young lady, please give your dad a message. Tell him thank you, and tell him that you are the first Americans to ever keep their promise!" Such powerful words.

Many years and shipments later, on one of our last visits to Cancer Hospital #62, Dr. Mahkson told my dad, "At first, I did not believe your faith. But I have seen it in action. I now accept your faith."

I mean, come on. Is there any greater example of the 1-2 punch? When we love people the way God has loved us, we earn the right to be heard. It's the combination of the punches that makes it most effective. When you truly love and know God, it's impossible to keep that love to yourself.

> "At first, I did not believe your faith. But I have seen it in action. I now accept your faith."

We all know the ultimate victory in a boxing match is a knockout. And in our case, the ultimate victory is knocking out the needs around the world. They say you don't need to be the most powerful puncher to knock someone out. You just need to land an accurate shot in the right place.

And I would add, you don't have to be the wealthiest person in the room to make a difference. You don't have to have all the answers to help save a life. You don't have to travel the globe and look directly into their eyes to feel and see their needs. All you have to do is put your energy behind this one small, strategic move—the 1-2 punch—making sure it lands in the right place.

By meeting the needs of the body and the soul together, we can knock out poverty, hunger, disease, and despair with a 1-2 punch.

With practical training and spiritual resources, we can help knock out slavery and oppression with a 1-2 punch.

With a bicycle, a soccer jersey, and a container of medical supplies, we can help save lives and spread the good news of the gospel far and wide.

"Both" is a 1-2 punch.

ALL THAT IS WHOLE IS HOLY

During my thirty years of humanitarian work, I've learned that in order to bring about wholeness in the world, you have to love people wholly. And that is holy work.

One partner wisely shared that, "Hunger has no religion."

Just think about it. If people don't have their basic needs met, how can they survive? And if they don't survive, do any of our other programs really matter? How can our strategies be effective if we can't even keep people alive?

As author Jamie Erickson points out, "Christ knew that a 'Go and sin no more' message would be drowned out by the rumbling of an empty stomach. So, Jesus multiplied fish and loaves. He satisfied physical needs before He met spiritual ones. And in the end, the former almost always paved the way for the latter."[8]

The truth is, when you feed the body, you feed the soul. And when you feed the soul, hope finally has the space to expand and flourish. And that's the strategy our partners of over three decades have repeated to us over and over.

---

8 Erickson, Jamie. Holy Hygge: Creating a Place for People to Gather and the Gospel to Grow, page 38.

I've witnessed it time and time again. When people have what they need to live another day, deeper hungers emerge. The hunger for belonging. The hunger for community. The hunger for God's Word and His ways.

Both hungers matter to God. Both hungers should matter to us.

Living out the meaning of both means embracing the beauty of paradox. And isn't that what faith is all about?

I believe Jesus modeled the "Genius of the AND." Think about it: He was God AND man. He preached faith AND works, truth-telling AND healing, justice AND mercy. Not only that, but He wanted everyone at the table—Jews AND Gentiles, rich AND poor, Pharisees AND prostitutes, children AND kings, friends AND enemies.

I believe the intent of the gospel is found in the AND. Help AND Hope. Always BOTH, and always with eternity in mind.

 Scan the QR code for photos, videos, and more details about the stories from around the world shared in this chapter.

CHAPTER FOUR / THE JUSTICE OF BOTH

THE JUDGE AND THE HUMANITARIAN

I sat in the back of the courtroom, trying not to be seen. I didn't want anyone to know I was the judge's wife, but I was also curious to find out what went down in this place where my husband spent so much of his time. What was it like? What was *he* like? And what would it feel like seeing him presiding over a courtroom?

My husband is a judge at the highest trial court level in the Commonwealth of Virginia. I have rarely witnessed him presiding over cases in his courtroom, but early in his career, I happened to stop by while he was advising a criminal defendant.

An advisement means informing the defendant of the charges against him and his right to counsel. When an individual is facing criminal charges that carry the possibility of jail time and cannot afford an attorney, the court will appoint a lawyer to represent that defendant.

As I watched my husband navigate through a series of required questions with the defendant, I was struck by how invasive, demeaning, and, well, just embarrassing these questions must be to an individual—especially in front of a courtroom full of strangers.

Are you employed? If so, how much do you make?

Do you have any assets (cash, bank accounts, motor vehicles, etc.)? If so, how much and what are they worth?

Do you own any real estate?

Do you receive any public assistance?

Do you have any outstanding financial obligations?

And so on.

I knew I could never ask anyone such private and personal questions. Yet, I was reminded of the many things my husband sees and deals with in a courtroom involving matters that simply seem out of bounds in normal everyday life. My husband kept his composure beautifully and behaved just like a judge should: calm, steady, compassionate, and fair.

And that is when I knew God had placed us in the right roles. Because if I had been in the judge's seat that day, I would have passed the defendant a note to meet me in the parking lot after court so I could hand him some money to help him get by.

I have often joked that my husband and I are on opposite ends of the justice spectrum. He is putting people in jail, and I am trying to get them out. But in all seriousness, to understand true justice, you have to look at it from both sides. A legal view of justice that punishes wrongdoing, and a biblical view of justice that rights wrongs and restores hope, allowing individuals to flourish. If you want to understand God's heart for His people, you have to consider both.

People have a lot to say about justice and injustice. The word "justice" immediately conjures up ideas and images from our own worldview, beliefs, and experiences.

Pastor and author Scott Sauls observed, "Younger generations are suspicious of biblical ethics. Older generations, of biblical justice. Jesus says you must have both if you are going to follow Him. Word AND deed. Grace AND truth. Love AND law. Ethics AND Justice. 'You must repent' AND 'remember the poor.'"[1]

In his book *Generous Justice*, Tim Keller explained it this way:

> *Some Christians believe that justice is strictly* misphat—*punishment of wrongdoing, period. This does not mean that they think that believers should be indifferent to the plight of the poor, but they would insist that helping the needy through generous giving should be called mercy, compassion, or charity, not justice. In English, however, the word 'charity' conveys a good but optional activity. Charity cannot be a requirement, for then it would not be charity. But this view does not fit in with the strength or balance of the biblical teaching.*
>
> *In the Scripture, gifts to the poor are called "acts of righteous-*

1 @scottsauls, "AND..." Instagram post, August 6, 2022. Accessed August 6, 2022. https://www.instagram.com/p/Cg7GuULux_w/?utm_source=ig_web_copy_link.

ness," as in Matthew 6:1–2. Not giving generously, then, is not stinginess, but unrighteousness, a violation of God's law. Also, we looked at Job's description of all the things he was doing in order to live a just and righteous life in Job 31. He calls every failure to help the poor a sin, offensive to God's splendor (verse 23) and deserving of judgment and punishment (verse 28). Remarkably, Job is asserting that it would be a sin against God to think of his goods as belonging to himself alone. To not "share his bread" and his assets with the poor would be unrighteous, a sin against God, and therefore by definition a violation of God's justice.[2]

To take this a step further, the words "charity" and "love" are often used interchangeably. In fact, the well-known verse found in 1 Corinthians 13:13 (KJV), reads, "And now abideth faith, hope, charity, these three; but the greatest of these is charity."[3] In most other translations, the word "love" is used in place of "charity."[4]

To separate justice and charity/love lets us off the hook too easily. Combining them makes us accountable. If your view of justice is simply a punishment for sin, then you also view charity as an optional activity. But a biblical view changes our understanding, and it should also change our response. When you view justice as a requirement to love and that denying charity, compassion, and sharing what we have with the poor is a violation of God's goodness, love, and fairness—well, that makes you look at things in a different way.

---

2 Timothy Keller, Generous Justice: How God's Grace Makes Us Just, Page 4

3 1 Cor. 13:13 (KJV)

4 1 Cor. 13:13 (NKJV, NIV, MSG, ESV)

At least it should. It should change the way we live. It should change the way we show up. It should change the way we look, act, and respond.

One of my favorite authors and pastors, Rich Villodas, says it this way: "The scandal of Christianity is that we love and encounter God through people, especially those on the margins of society, the edges of our awareness, or the 'wrong' side of a conflict (an 'enemy'). If the love we claim to have doesn't lead to a commitment to seeing wholeness and justice, we will have short-circuited God's love."[5]

To deny God's justice is also denying His love. It is both.

THE RHYTHM OF THE KINGDOM

In the well-known parable of the Good Samaritan, Jesus links the greatest commandments—loving God and loving your neighbor as yourself—to the concept of addressing injustice.

You probably have heard this story many times throughout your life. But that familiarity can also mean that we begin to miss the main point and the very essence of this timeless lesson.

Jesus teaches that when the priest and the Levite pass by on the other side of the road to avoid the beaten man, they truly abandon their "neighbor" in a traditional sense and leave him for dead.

But the Samaritan stopped.

5 Rich Villodas, Good and Beautiful and Kind: Becoming Whole in a Fractured World, page 182.

Culturally, this man should not have mattered to the Samaritan because they were enemies. In this historical context, the Samaritan knew the man he was helping viewed him as racially inferior—and most likely, a religious heretic. It would have been socially acceptable for the Samaritan to leave this man to die.

> Because in the eyes of Christ, anyone in need is our neighbor—no exceptions.

But instead, he helped. Because in the eyes of Christ, anyone in need is our neighbor—no exceptions. And how did the Samaritan help? He bandaged the injured man's wounds, carried him on his donkey, found him lodging, and paid his expenses.

To me, there is so much to learn from this well-known story if we just sit with it for a minute. I believe this parable challenges us to expand our definition of love to encompass the needs of the whole person. The Good Samaritan loved his neighbor by addressing his immediate physical and economic needs. Jesus illustrates that helping others is not a means to an end; it is an end itself.

And it also demonstrates that we can love regardless of whether or not people are good because God is good. For Jesus, this generous, sacrificial love is among the greatest instruments of justice.

I believe the greatest injustice we face is hopelessness. Why? Because time after time, I've seen that justice is what unlocks hope. As the author of the book turned film, *Just Mercy*, Bryan Stevenson says, "It's not a pie in the sky hope, it's not a preference for optimism over pessimism. It's an orientation of the spirit. I think hopelessness is the enemy of justice. Injustice prevails where hopelessness persists. And so, hope is our requirement, it's our superpower."[6]

Our superpower. I love that. Who doesn't want to be a superhero or at least have one superhero-like quality. And the good news is we do, if only we will use it.

> **Love. Justice. Hope. That is the rhythm of the kingdom of God.**

My favorite part of this parable is the end. The religious expert realizes the one who was the true neighbor was the one who had mercy on the beaten man. And then in just four powerful words, Jesus tells us exactly what to do: "Go and do likewise."[7] I read once that these four words have the power to change the world.[8]

And here is how:

> Love God. Love your neighbor.
>
> Seek justice for your neighbor—physical and spiritual.
>
> That justice will unlock hope.
>
> That hope has the power to change the world.
>
> Love. Justice. Hope.
>
> That is the rhythm of the kingdom of God.

---

6 Bryan Stevenson, "A Quote from Just Mercy," Goodreads, accessed June 16, 2023, https://www.goodreads.com/quotes/9785927-t-he-only-thing-they-needed-was-hope-not-that-pie.

7 Luke 10:37 (ESV)

8 Tetsunao Yamamori. The Hope Factor: Engaging the Church in the HIV/AIDS Crisis , Page 264.

NEVER AGAIN

"Forever let this place be a cry of despair and a warning to humanity."[9]

Those words can be found on a memorial plaque on the grounds of Auschwitz in Poland, the largest of the German Nazi concentration camps and an extermination center. My first time to Auschwitz was profound. I was overwhelmed by the evidence of such evil on full display. And I was overwhelmed by the responsibility of the words "never again."

I had been to the Holocaust Museum in Washington D.C., but nothing compares to standing on the grounds of Auschwitz. As I anticipated my first visit, I thought I might be emotional. But instead of tears, I simply felt anger boiling up inside.

The train tracks were what got me. I had just seen pictures of the masses of people crammed into the trains and unloaded at this very spot. I saw photos of where they were divided into two lines. One line headed to forced labor, the other headed to the gas chamber. And standing where those people actually lined up along the tracks was haunting.

I visited Auschwitz three times in a matter of months. I don't recommend that by the way. But it did give me a chance to process what I was seeing. It gave me a chance to ask different questions. It gave me a chance to question if we have really come that far at all.

It seems unimaginable. Surreal. How could something like this

9 Bryan Stevenson, "A Quote from Just Mercy," Goodreads, accessed June 16, 2023, https://www.goodreads.com/quotes/9785927-t-he-only-thing-they-needed-was-hope-not-that-pie.

ever happen? That is what's so devastating about the Holocaust—it wasn't a natural disaster or an accident or a terrible oversight. In order for millions of Jews to die in the gas chambers, millions of other people had to go about business as usual. So many had to remain silent. So many had to look the other way. So many had to simply "follow orders" or ignore the smokestacks of the crematoriums in their own towns.

> **In order for millions of Jews to die in the gas chambers, millions of other people had to go about business as usual.**

Most recently, we have seen the images of the war in Ukraine, and we have heard the stories in real time. And yet, as much as we use the words "never forget," it seems we may have done just that.

I have heard differing opinions on comparing the atrocities of World War II to the war in Ukraine. But it was impossible to not feel the heaviness and find the similarities as I stood there, knowing that just miles down the road people were fleeing across the border, running for their lives.

On my second visit, I met two young women from Ukraine. They work with our partners on the ground in both Ukraine and Poland. And hearing about the war from their perspective forever changed me.

At the time, there was much debate over what to call or how to define what was happening in Ukraine. Some called it a conflict. Some, an invasion. And others, a humanitarian crisis. But to my new friends, there was no confusion. They said it is *war*. And to call it anything else is to add insult to injury—to condescendingly say to all Ukrainians that things are just "not that bad."

There is no debate for the people living through this "crisis" on how to define it. Some even refer to it as genocide. And that is why walking the grounds of Auschwitz with those two young women made me feel a bit different.

As we stood where so many had lost their lives, one of the young women compared the debate about the Ukrainian war with a girl being raped. She said it is like trying to share the blame of that attack because the victim's skirt was too short.

And if that doesn't get your attention, then I don't know what will. It stopped me in my tracks.

Ukrainians hear of their countrymen being taken to "camps" in Russia for resisting the war and takeover. There are reports of children being kidnapped, taken from their families, and tortured by telling them their families have abandoned them. There are mass graves and evidence of genocide. So you can see how a visit to Auschwitz would trigger so many emotions for these two women.

The Ukrainian people want peace. But peace is unattainable when an aggressor is determined to wipe them out. And the haunting questions I keep asking myself: How long do we wait? How many people have to die before we define this for what it is? How many more people have to flee, leaving everything they own and love behind?

At the time of this writing, millions of people have fled, and their entire lives have been turned upside down.[10]

And to say *never again* means we cannot stay silent. We cannot sit back and do nothing.

Think about it: history's most unthinkable atrocities were possible because, to paraphrase philosopher Edmund Burke, "good people did nothing." They didn't kill or persecute or enslave or starve. They didn't hate. They did worse—they were indifferent.

Holocaust survivor Elie Wiesel wrote, "The opposite of love is not hate, it's indifference. The opposite of art is not ugliness, it's indifference. The opposite of faith is not heresy, it's indifference. And the opposite of life is not death, it's indifference."[11]

Good, ordinary people stood by for centuries during the kidnapping and forced labor of millions of men, women, and children.

Good, ordinary people raised their voices in worship to God to drown out the haunting sounds of their countrymen being murdered by the Nazis.

Good, ordinary people in good, ordinary churches failed to report child abuse to the authorities because they feared it would threaten those in power who, after all, were busy saving souls.

Good, ordinary people—just like you and me—can turn the TV

---

10 "Ukraine Emergency: Aid, Statistics and News: USA FOR UNHCR," Ukraine Emergency: Aid, Statistics and News | USA for UNHCR, accessed May 5, 2023, https://www.unrefugees.org/emergencies/ukraine/#:~:text=There%20are%20 an%20estimated%205%2C914%2C000%20internally%20displaced%20people%20in%20Ukraine.&text=Nearly%20 8%20million%20refugees%20from,neighboring%20countries%20and%20across%20Europe.&text=Approximately%20 17.6%20million%20people%20are%20in%20need%20of%20humanitarian%20assistance%20in%202023.

11 "One Must Not Forget," interview by Alvin P. Sanoff, US News & World Report (Oct. 27, 1986.)

channel the moment we see upsetting images of refugee families going hungry because, after all, they don't share our faith.

Good, ordinary people can allow terrible things. And good, ordinary people can also change the world.

THE LAST WORD

During the worst moments of the 1994 Rwandan Genocide, between 800,000 to 1 million people were killed in 100 days. Most were hacked to death with machetes. Neighbor turned on neighbor. Villages lay strewn with bodies. The massacre, ignited by ethnic division and carried out by the Hutu majority, mostly against the Tutsi minority, rocked this tiny nation and sent shockwaves across the world.

Good, ordinary people can allow terrible things. And good, ordinary people can also change the world.

The global community—as it did when the Holocaust first ushered the word "genocide" into our vocabulary—vowed, one more time, to "never again" let something like this happen.

But sadly, genocide still rages on today. Still, there is hope and lessons to be learned from the people who have lived through it.

There is something about Rwanda—this land of a thousand hills. I can't describe it, but the forgiveness and redemption that permeate this country is irresistible. Author Jonathan Golden says that "Rwanda is the kind of place you go when you doubt

God's existence and need to rekindle your faith."[12] To me, it is a place flowing with God's grace and a reminder that the same grace is offered to us each and every day.

In an opinion piece I wrote for *The Christian Post*, I observed that "barely two decades after the genocide, Rwanda is now a prosperous country with regional influence in Africa. Between 2001 and 2014, it boasted one of the fastest-growing economies on the continent. International technology companies are investing and creating jobs in Rwanda. The streets of Kigali, the capital, are clean and transited by smart buses equipped with free 4G wireless internet. Child mortality has dropped by two-thirds. In five short years, the national poverty rate dropped by 14 percent. Literacy rates, enrollment in primary education, and health care availability have risen. And perhaps most shocking, perpetrators and survivors of the bloody days of 1994 now live together in peace—their children even intermarry.

"According to the United Nations, to establish swift justice for the thousands accused of committing genocide, the Rwandan government reopened the country's traditional court system known as "Gacaca." Trials were conducted by locally elected judges, and lower sentences were granted if the defendant repented and tried to reconcile with the community. Forgiveness was asked for and granted publicly, establishing unwritten—yet commonly held and understood—social expectations from the community and the perpetrators."[13]

One of the most fascinating outcomes of the Gacaca courts

---

12 Jonathan David Golden, Be You. Do Good. Page 18

13 Yeatts, Noel. "How to Recover from Genocide? What Iraq can Learn from Rwanda."
The Christian Post, Sept. 26, 2016. https://www.christianpost.com/news/how-to-recover-from-genocide-what-iraq-can-learn-from-rwanda-169995/#zJelWdJU4wTUbUkh.99

was the responsibility given to perpetrators to not only serve a sentence, but to also do good to their victims. A Hutu man who had killed a Tutsi woman's husband would come back and help rebuild her house. Cases like these helped Rwanda find reconciliation where no one else thought it possible.

I stood in a valley outside of Kigali where blood once flowed. But like so much of Rwanda, forgiveness has transformed this valley from a place of death to a place of life. Tools once used to take lives are now used to produce crops and raise livestock. Former enemies proudly work side by side despite their past. Most of the women lost their husbands in the genocide. But today, it does not matter what side they were once on; all that matters is their future. This is reinforced by the literal translation of their village's name, "do something with your life," and their sheer determination to do just that.

> ... forgiveness has transformed this valley from a place of death to a place of life.

Marian's husband died in the genocide. Besides her spouse, she lost eight family members including her sister and father Before he died, her husband contracted HIV and passed it to Marian. She now lives in a co-op community with other women who have experienced great loss. She told us that being with others helped give her hope. She said she never gave up on God, and even now she is still praying, and she still has faith.

Elise is the man who helps run this co-op with the survivors. His father, who was also killed in the genocide, had been in the hospital when the militia came looking for men to fight. When they found that his father was physically not able to join them, they smashed his head against the wall.

Just miles down the road is another village full of genocide survivors. We call it the widows' village. After losing their husbands, the women all needed a home. The government provided forty-five homes for these widows and their children.

And now years later, a new generation of children is living in this village. World Help supporters sponsor the children here and help them attend school nearby. And on one of my visits, we were able to help provide clean water for this community.

But meeting the women here is something you just can't forget. They showed me the scars still visible on their bodies from machetes—proof of their horrific past.

Aloisy's husband was killed along with three of her children. As she ran to escape, her foot was severely cut by a machete. She still has the scar as a vivid reminder.

Melida was chased from her house and ran to the forest, but she was still attacked with machetes. She was barely alive when neighbors who witnessed the assault came to her rescue and helped hide her. An ugly scar on her neck is a souvenir from that terrifying day.

But as shocking as these stories are, what is more unbelievable is the way these ethnic groups have found reconciliation and peace. Both Hutus and Tutsis live together in this village. Forgiveness has transformed this community, just like it has in so many other villages. Former combatants are living in harmony despite their past.

In the end, only reconciliation and forgiveness can bind up a nation after genocide. Through pain and perseverance, Rwanda is conquering its dark past.

Genocide, it seems, does not always get the last word. And neither does injustice.

THE LOVE OF JUSTICE

The fact that God sent His Son to earth to be born, to live the human experience, and even to suffer tells us something about the value of this up-close kind of love. Jesus didn't just sympathize with the marginalized; He was one of them. He was poor. He was without social standing, power, or material possessions.

Jesus didn't just tend to the lonely, the scorned, and the falsely accused as an exercise of pity. He was lonely, He was scorned, and He was sinless yet brutally tortured and killed at the hands of the state.

His identification with the downtrodden and the vulnerable wasn't performative. It wasn't sentimental or syrupy sweet. It was a dangerous contradiction with radical social implications: a God who suffered, a God who wept, a God who was on eye level with injustice.

Instead of claiming the power and authority that was rightly His, Jesus moved into the worst neighborhoods and found love, goodness, and humanity there. He not only lifted up the vulnerable, but He also allowed Himself to become vulnerable—Immanuel, God with us.

Scott Sauls puts it this way: "To talk about Jesus and be silent about justice misses so very much concerning Jesus. To talk about justice and be silent about Jesus misses so very much concerning justice."[14]

Jesus didn't just sympathize with the marginalized; He was one of them.

The world desperately needs this "seeing" kind of love. It's the only way we can really begin to bring help and hope to those in need. We have to look. We have to see. We have to get closer. And we have to act.

Perhaps the way Cornel West, professor, author, and activist, describes it is true: "Justice is what love looks like in public."[15]

And in order to show the world this kind of love, we need God's power to make right what has been wrong.

Wrong things right.

That is true justice.

We have seen time and time again that righting a wrong requires more than finding a perpetrator. It requires more than a conviction. It requires more than bringing people to "justice" to pay for their crimes.

14 Sauls, Scott (@scottsauls). "To talk about Jesus and be silent about justice misses so very much concerning Jesus." Twitter January 7, 2023. https://twitter.com/scottsauls/status/1611826545508728832?s=20\

15 West, Cornel. 2010. "Never forget that justice is what love looks like in public." October 28, 2010. https://www.facebook.com/drcornelwest/posts/never-forget-that-justice-is-what-love-looks-like-inpublic/119696361424073/

That is only the immediate help. But the long-term hope comes from true transformation.

In the debate over what true justice really is, I love how pastor Louie Giglio explains it:

> *We care about justice and the poor because it would be a tragedy if we gave the next generation the impression that worship is just about singing more songs. Worship is about doing justice and reaching out to the lost and least of these in Jesus's name.* ***Worship and justice are two sides of the same coin.***[16]

And once again, the answer is found in both. The humanitarian AND the evangelist. Worship AND compassion. Justice AND love. The beauty of both.

---

16 Drew Dyck, "Louie Giglio: Passion for a Generation-Part 2," outreachmagazine.com, April 22, 2016, https://outreachmagazine.com/interviews/16583-louie-giglio-passion-for-a-generation-part-2.htm

 Scan the QR code for photos, videos, and more details about the stories from around the world shared in this chapter.

CHAPTER FIVE / THE KINGDOM OF BOTH

WHAT A FRIEND

I looked around the school auditorium at the overwhelming mounds of donated clothes and piles of shoes. Displaced Ukrainians who flooded through these doors arrived with little more than the clothes on their backs. This place allowed them the freedom to choose what they needed.

Crossing the border into Ukraine during the summer of 2022—months into the Russian invasion that sent millions fleeing for their lives—was a surreal moment. Knowing that I was in a country ripped apart by war was unsettling and something I would never forget.

We drove to a high school where our partners were working. Schools had been closed since the war broke out, but part of this school had been repurposed as a refugee center for those displaced by the conflict. When I was there, it was home to about 230 people—mostly women and children. Another part of the school was being used to make bulletproof vests. During my visit, the children were still receiving three meals a day; the adults, however, were down to one meal a day. They simply were running out of resources.

I met Marina and her two young granddaughters. They fled their home shortly after the war began and had been at the center for three months. They left behind a husband, father, and other family members. They lived near Bucha, the area now known for atrocities that have been called genocide. I asked Marina what it was like to hear that news. She just began to cry. I can't even imagine hearing about such evil in your hometown and being helpless to stop it.

> When Ukrainian refugees began to flee across the border into Romania, this church didn't avoid the situation. They didn't walk the other way. They didn't turn a blind eye.

Her granddaughters were sweet and playful. They missed their father but were happy they got to bring their dog with them. Before we finished, I asked Marina what her biggest needs were. She said more than anything she wished for peace in Ukraine and to go home and be reunited with her family.

I still marvel at a church of thirty-five people I visited just on the other side of the border in Romania. Even with few members, this congregation was making an incredible difference.

When Ukrainian refugees began to flee across the border into

Romania, this church didn't avoid the situation. They didn't walk the other way. They didn't turn a blind eye.

Instead, they took in *more than seventy people*—five large families made up of sets of parents and their sixty biological and foster children. One family alone had eighteen children. These boys and girls, who came from a children's home in Ukraine, were already among the most vulnerable. Many had been separated from their biological families and now were made to leave their home as well.

These families stayed in the church basement at first, until members could help find them housing in the community. The small congregation continued to feed and care for them at the church. I visited some of these families in their new homes, donated and shared by the Romanian church.

A group of Americans accompanied me on one of my visits. After meeting with the families, we were invited to worship together in that tiny church, now bursting at the seams but full of hope. The pastor led the church in a familiar hymn as the piano began to play. I knew I recognized the song, but I just couldn't place it at first.

In his booming voice, he said, "In Romanian." And suddenly the beautiful voices of those thirty-five members started singing an old hymn I knew but had not sung in some time.

What a friend we have in Jesus,
All our sins and griefs to bear!
What a privilege to carry
Everything to God in prayer!

Then he said, "In Ukrainian." And the voices of those seventy-four refugees, who had just fled for their lives, filled the room.

Oh, what peace we often forfeit,
Oh, what needless pain we bear,
All because we do not carry
Everything to God in prayer.

Then, "In American." My team of ten panicked and rushed to pull up the lyrics on their phones. None of us had sung this hymn in quite some time. One friend even whispered, "I think this is an Alan Jackson song." *Nope,* I thought. *Pretty sure this is a hymn.*

We pulled ourselves together and started to sheepishly sing whatever lyrics we could find.

Have we trials and temptations?
Is there trouble anywhere?
We should never be discouraged,
Take it to the Lord in prayer.

And in one moment . . . in one tiny, Romanian church . . . the nations came together. And it was powerful.

The origins of this hymn are believed to be a poem written in the nineteenth century by a struggling immigrant named Joseph Scriven. His life was marked by tragedy—losing not one, but two fiancées who passed before he could marry them. He took a vow of poverty and devoted his life to working with the poor and less fortunate. He was even named "The Good Samaritan of Port Hope" where he lived in Canada.

Other scholars believe Scriven originally sent the poem, that would one day become a famous hymn, to his mother who was dying far away in another country.[1]

> Refugees all around me were also struggling to find their way in another country. They had left loved ones behind. They had lost loved ones. And yet, what a friend. What a friend we have in Jesus.

I couldn't help but relate that origin story to what I witnessed in church that day. Refugees all around me were also struggling to find their way in another country. They had left loved ones behind. They had lost loved ones. And yet, what a friend. What a friend we have in Jesus.

French theologian John Calvin once said, "We must make the invisible kingdom visible in our midst."[2] On that day in a little Romanian church near the southern border of Ukraine, the kingdom was more visible to me than it has ever been.

SET THE WORLD RIGHT

"There is no news."

On April 18, 1930, the British Broadcasting Corporation declared there was no news to report that day. No news! And instead, they filled the rest of their radio segment with peaceful piano music.

1 Hawn, Michael. "History of Hymns: 'What a Friend We Have in Jesus'." Discipleship Ministries, February 3, 2021. https://www.umcdiscipleship.org/articles/history-of-hymns-what-a-friend-we-have-in-jesus

2 "Quotes by John Calvin." Grace Quotes, June 30, 2021. https://gracequotes.org/author-quote/john-calvin/

Can you imagine a day where there is no news? That's certainly not our world today.

I look at the mess happening around the globe. The darkness of the sex industry in India and Thailand. The extreme poverty in Guatemala and Uganda. The lack of Bibles in Cuba. The persecution of Christians in North Korea. War and humanitarian disasters. The never-ending political debates and divisiveness. The reckoning of Christian leaders entrenched in scandals and hypocrisy. And I think, *Wouldn't it be nice to just clean this all up? Wouldn't it be nice to simply give some helpful tips and walk away feeling like it was all fixed?*

> I believe our faith should give us the desire to restore hope and bring God's kingdom to life here on earth—to set the world right—not in the future, but now.

I can't help but be reminded of a familiar phrase in Luke, which is part of the Lord's Prayer. In the King James Version it reads, "Thy kingdom come. Thy will be done, as in heaven, so in earth."[3]

This is how I always heard it growing up. But I'm partial to the Message version: "Our Father in heaven, reveal who you are.

Set the world right; Do what's best—as above, so below."

Set the world right.

---

3 Luke 11:2-4 (KJV)

While I am outraged by the injustices we face in our world, I know that God is even more outraged and more grieved. But while He is sorting out all the brokenness in the world, I believe He is also calling us to help Him put things right and to restore hope.

In his book, *Good, Beautiful, and Kind*, Rich Villodas explains that "When Jesus taught his disciples to pray, he instructed them to say, 'Your kingdom come, your will be done, on earth as it is in heaven' (Matthew 6:10). Is that not love? Is that not justice? To pray these words is not to passively say, 'Lord, there's nothing we can do, so please fix this world.' Rather, the Lord's Prayer calls us to say, 'Lord, there's so much we can do, but only ever in your power.'"[4]

I believe our faith should give us the desire to restore hope and bring God's kingdom to life here on earth—to set the world right—not in the future, but now. That's why I love these words from Anglican author Ted Schroder:

> *What do we mean when we pray, "Thy will be done on earth as it is in heaven?" We are praying that something will happen that has not yet happened. We are praying that God will bring about his heavenly purpose on earth. We are praying that God would use us to do his will. We are making ourselves available to do the will of our heavenly Father, to fulfill his purpose.*
>
> *Praying for the will of God to be done in and through our lives on earth, as it is in heaven, means that we are willing to go through whatever might prevent that purpose from being accomplished.*

4 Rich Villodas, Good and Beautiful and Kind: Becoming Whole in a Fractured World, page 202.

Our prayer is that we want to be so aligned with the will and purpose of God that we ask God to empower us to accomplish it. The prayer is a battle-cry in the struggle to bring about God's purposes on earth.

We are praying that we and others might be the means whereby God's purpose might be accomplished: that the justice and peace of God's kingdom will become a reality in people's lives.[5]

Set the world right.

NEW KINGDOM PEOPLE

Jesus's new kingdom has old roots.

It wasn't a new idea. It wasn't God's Plan B. It was a renovation of God's original vision for humans flourishing from the beginning.

Like theologian N.T. Wright says: "Redemption doesn't mean scrapping what's there and starting again from a clean slate, but rather liberating what has become enslaved."[6]

Anyone who has ever done home remodeling knows this on a fundamental level. You're choosing to restore, to work with what you have to create something better. You have to understand that restoration is a risk. It's a long-term investment with long-term goals.

5 Ted Schroder, "Your Will Be Done on Earth as It Is in Heaven: Virtueonline – The Voice for Global Orthodox Anglicanism," VirtueOnline, May 1, 2005, https://virtueonline.org/your-will-be-done-earth-it-heaven.

6 NT Wright, Surprised by Hope: Rethinking Heaven, the Resurrection, and the Mission of the Church, page 96.

In the Sermon on the Mount, Jesus laid out the counter cultural conditions of His reign—a vision of what a "just" world could mean for those who have been left out:

> *Blessed are the poor in spirit. Blessed are those who mourn. Blessed are the meek. Blessed are those who are persecuted. Blessed are those who hunger and thirst for righteousness.*[7]

Did you catch that? "Blessed" becomes the first name of new kingdom citizens. Jesus's kingdom values are a complete rejection of "the way things are." Who's "on top" in God's kingdom? Those whom the world forgets, diminishes, and marginalizes.

The Sermon on the Mount was an outright rejection of the values that much of the ancient world prized: power, might, and domination. The weak were conquered and subdued by the strong.

> **Jesus's kingdom values are a complete rejection of "the way things are." Who's "on top" in God's kingdom? Those whom the world forgets, diminishes, and marginalizes.**

It was as if He were saying to the powers that be, "I won't play by your rules." Jesus didn't come to earth to build a country club. He came to build a kingdom where the last shall be first.

In fact, it's pretty hard to find examples in the Bible where Jesus did not meet people right where they were. And their physical needs were always important to Him. Feeding the 5,000, giving sight to the blind man—even raising people from the dead. This was not an afterthought or only if He had time; it was a priority. Jesus met people wherever they happened to be in their spiritual journey and in ways they could understand.

Pastor and author Eugene Cho posted similar thoughts, contending that, "In His last days, Jesus didn't just enter Jerusalem and go straight to the cross. In between, He confronts corruption and hypocrisy, overturns tables, heals the blind and sick, feeds people, and washes dirty feet. In other words, following Jesus isn't just about a ticket to heaven. On earth as in heaven."[8]

> May we be a people who not only pray the Lord's Prayer—for God to "set the world right"—but be a people who join Him in setting the world right.

Jesus had compassion.

One of our favorite sayings around World Help is, "Pity sees and even feels, but compassion touches the need. Compassion requires action."[9]

Jesus—the very one who could heal the entire world of all its pain with a single word—chose to devote His life to twelve disciples and a handful of outcasts. Seeing the one—the person right in front of Him in need—wasn't just important to Him; it was the way He changed the world!

When we consider the life of Jesus—from His intimate iden-

8 @eugenecho, "On earth as it is in heaven. Amen." Instagram Post. April 12, 2022. Accessed April 12, 2022. https://www.instagram.com/p/CcQ_s6xvHJn/?igshid=MDJmNzVkMjY%3D

9 Anonymous

tification with the marginalized to the imagining of a new law that is fulfilled through the sacrificial love for our neighbors—it is apparent the kingdom He is building is here among us *now.* Yet, it will not be complete until His return. And the Great Commission is our "deployment," if you will, of the new kingdom.

It's easy to look at the darkness in this world and want to run and hide. But as Christ-followers, that isn't the life we are called to live. We aren't the people who turn a blind eye to suffering and bury our heads in the sand when we hear of refugees fleeing for their lives or babies dying from starvation.

May we be a people who not only pray the Lord's Prayer—for God to "set the world right"—but be a people who join Him in *setting the world right.*

Do you dream for a better world?

To you I say: Blessed are the dreamers, for theirs is the faith that imagines what is possible before it is probable.

Do you long to heal the sick and feed the hungry?

To you, I say: Blessed are the healers, for theirs is the gift that saves bodies and souls.

Do you want to seek justice for the oppressed?

To you, I say: Blessed are the freedom fighters, for theirs is liberation for the oppressed.

Do you want to give generously of your time, talent, or resources to help people in need?

To you, I say: Blessed are the risk-takers, for theirs is the God of the impossible.

Do you want to make a difference in this world that will outlive you?

To us, I say: Blessed are we, new kingdom people, for ours is the hope that will not disappoint.

 Scan the QR code for photos, videos, and more details about the stories from around the world shared in this chapter.

CHAPTER SIX / THE GOOD NEWS OF BOTH

SALVATION DOESN'T STAY STILL

She was considered "untouchable."

Born into the lowest tier of the caste system, "D" was despised by everyone. She had been a professional witch for forty years. When she wasn't practicing her dark magic, she was persecuting Christians. Her heart was filled with hatred. She often thought about how she would love to wipe out all the Christians in her village.

When the pandemic struck, D and her three sons lost their jobs. She didn't know how she was going to survive. Her family went several days without any food at all.

Then one day a visitor came by her house. She recognized him as a local pastor whom she frequently abused verbally. But before she could start berating and insulting him, he gave her a bag of food to help meet her needs. D was blown away.

She later said, "I never thought of getting support from the people I persecuted. But Christians reached out to us unconditionally when we needed help desperately."

D accepted Christ, stopped practicing witchcraft, and immediately started telling other people about God. Because of D's testimony, eight families came to Christ, and thirty-two new people joined the local church! Isn't that amazing?

> Salvation doesn't stay still because it can't! It makes everything and everyone around it grow.

It makes me think of the gospel accounts where Jesus casts out demons or heals someone. Out of sheer joy, they immediately start running around, telling everyone they see about what He had done. Why?

Because what Jesus gave them was so miraculous, so incredible, and so captivating that it was too much to keep inside. That's how it is with salvation; it may start with an individual's decision to repent and to follow Christ, but it never stops there.

Accepting Christ unleashes an inner freedom that can't help but make itself known. Salvation animates a person's life in a way that wasn't possible before. Instead of marking a solitary event along a timeline, salvation, instead, serves as a catalyst for a deeper, ongoing transformation—bleeding across the lines we draw and coloring every moment in hues of grace. Salvation doesn't stay still because it can't! It makes everything and everyone around it grow.

Author Sarah Bessey describes what happens next:

> *Once we become disciples of Jesus, we live in the Kingdom of God. And we cannot separate our salvation into a private event, divorced from what Darrell Guder calls the 'advent of God's healing reign over all the world.' Ours is a distinct calling—to demonstrate the reality of God's redemptive power in the world today.*[1]

The early Christians, for example, certainly didn't consider salvation to be a private, polite event. They understood they were not being called to play by the rules. Their salvation gave them the courage to refuse to bend to the cruelty being practiced all around them. Their faith was disobedient, defiant, and foolish because it signaled that a new kingdom—Jesus's kingdom where the last shall be first—was the only one that mattered.

I love Jesus's parable that illustrates this idea so vividly. It is only two sentences:

"The kingdom of heaven is like treasure hidden in a field. When a man found it, he hid it again, and then in his joy went and sold all he had and bought that field."[2]

In the words of John Piper, "The kingdom of God is so valuable that losing everything on earth, but getting the kingdom, is a happy trade-off."[3]

Like the people Jesus healed, and like the early Christians, D knew she had everything to gain by telling others about what

---

1 Sarah Bessey, Jesus Feminist, page 161.

2 Matthew 13:34 (NIV)

3 Piper, John. "The Kingdom of Heaven Is a Treasure." Desiring God, February 21, 2023. https://www.desiringgod.org/messages/the-kingdom-of-heaven-is-a-treasure.

God had done in her life. She had found her treasure in a field, her "happy trade-off" of becoming a citizen of a new kingdom rather than clinging to the old one. And she couldn't keep the good news to herself for a second longer.

> # The gospel is good. So good, in fact, that it belongs not only to us as individuals, but also to the world.

Stories like D's remind me that the genius of the gospel is its multidimensionality—it's both-ness in spectrum and effect. An encounter with the gospel holds us steady, and at the same time, dares us to move out of complacency. The gospel satisfies us with grace while nurturing within us a relentless hunger and thirst for righteousness. The gospel is devastating in its clarity and comforting in its power. The gospel isn't safe, or small, or simplistic, or monochromatic. *The gospel is good.* So good, in fact, that it belongs not only to us as individuals, but also to the world.

GOOD NEWS FOR THE WORLD

Jordan Raynor, in his devotional series, "Beyond Saving Souls," points something out that has stayed with me:

"In the Gospels, Jesus used the word 'save' or 'saved' *less than 10 times.* By contrast, he referred to his coming 'Kingdom' *more than 150 times.*"

He goes on to say,

In our churches today, we talk a lot about saving souls, and very little about what Jesus called 'the Kingdom of God.' This is

*startling because it is the exact opposite of what we see Jesus em-
phasizing in the New Testament. In Matthew 24:14, Jesus said
that it is the 'gospel of the Kingdom' that 'will be preached in the
whole world,' not the gospel of individual salvation. The gospel
is not just good news for our souls, it is good news for the world.*[4]

Did you hear that? The gospel is not just good news for our
souls, it is good news for the *world*.

He goes on to quote Tim Keller, who said, "The ultimate purpose of Jesus is not only individual salvation and pardon for sins
but also the renewal of this world, the end of disease, poverty,
injustice, violence, suffering, and death."

This, in a nutshell, is why I do the work I do every day. It's why
World Help exists.

You see, I believe that
salvation is not a winning
lottery ticket that we get
to keep and give away to a
select few. Salvation is an

Because the gospel is good news for the world.

invitation for transformation—present and active and ongoing
transformation. Transformation that awakens a yearning inside
of us to restore all that sin has displaced and disrupted.

It only makes sense that a person who has been rescued from
spiritual poverty and destitution would be equally compelled to
seek justice for the physical, emotional, and spiritual poverty of
their neighbors.

---

4 Jordan Raynor, "Beyond Saving Souls," YouVersion | The Bible App | Bible.com, accessed June 13, 2023,
https://www.bible.com/reading-plans/20539-beyond-saving-souls.

When we recognize the grace that has been extended to us, we understand that the kingdom is worth our time, our talents, and our resources. It's worth everything. When we experience freedom, we bet it all. Because we want everyone around us to experience it too. *Because the gospel is good news for the world.*

A WORLD-SHIFTING MOVEMENT

Again, the early Christians have a lot to teach us about this idea. In those days, Jesus had instructed His followers to step out of line of the culture. This meant the early Christians didn't just love in theory, but in life, in work, and in community. This love didn't solely exist among themselves, but it also radiated to the sick, the elderly, the poor, the destitute, and even, inexplicably, to their enemies.

Even though it was dangerous to practice Christianity openly, it was extremely attractive to many, particularly the oppressed and vulnerable—those whose lives mattered very little in this earthly, man-ruled kingdom.

In Jesus's kingdom, they all had seats at the table. And despite the rampant persecution and killings of Christians under the Roman Empire, their numbers continued to grow into a world-shifting movement.

The historian Rodney Stark describes the wide-reaching effects of the early Christians' social and cultural disruption:

> *Christians revitalized life in Greco-Roman cities by providing new norms and new kinds of social relationships able to cope with*

many urgent urban problems. To cities filled with the homeless, impoverished, and strangers, Christians offered an immediate basis for attachments. To cities filled with orphans and widows, Christians provided a new and expanded sense of family. To cities torn by violent ethnic strife, Christians offered a new basis for social solidarity. And to cities faced with epidemic, fires and earthquakes, Christians offered effective nursing services. Thus, the early Christians ministered as a transformative movement that arose in response to the misery, chaos, fear and brutality of life in the Roman Empire.[5]

Christianity's greatest offense was not that it was a new religion among many others. It wasn't the theories or the doctrines or the do's and don'ts. It was that the Christians' beliefs actually compelled them to live in a completely counter cultural and disruptive way.

I love this verse in 1 Thessalonians where Paul is writing to the church and telling them about how contagious their way of life has been. He says:

Do you know that all over the provinces . . . believers look up to you? The word has gotten around. Your lives are echoing the Master's Word, not only in the provinces but all over the place. The news of your faith in God is out. We don't even have to say anything anymore—you're the message![6]

That last part gets me: *You're the message.*

---

5 Rodney Stark, The Rise of Christianity: How the Obscure, Marginal Jesus Movement Became the Dominant Religious Force in the Western World in a Few Centuries. page 160-161.

6 1 Thessalonians 1:7-10 (MSG)

While most of us—especially in America—aren't attempting to share the gospel under pain of death, we are still living through some crazy times.

Poverty, war, greed, polarization, hatred, disease, hopelessness, and in recent years, a global pandemic. If you're paying any kind of attention, it's impossible not to know what's happening.

We hear it on the news. We see it on our screens. We feel it all around us. We're all thinking: *None of this is normal. This is not how things ought to be.*

During the pandemic, I heard several commentators describe the time as "apocalyptic." That word has always made me think of collapse and chaos, but it turns out that in Greek, the word actually means an *unveiling*.[7]

Although the word conjures for us cinematic images of destroyed cities and secret bunkers, the energy of an apocalypse is more generative than it is destructive. Its arrival unleashes a revelation of knowledge and truths previously unknown—which is an eerily precise description of the pandemic's unmasking effect.

A crisis, in fact, is great at uncovering our assumptions—what we thought was stable, what we normalized without question, and whom we claimed to know from a distance. It scrubs all pretense and disguise of the stark inequalities experienced by so many in our world; that is, if we're willing to look.

When you think about how the pandemic affected our lives, you could say that it certainly created new problems we had nev-

---

7 Meajor Eric, "Apocalyptic of Daniel and Revelation," Academia.edu, March 17, 2017, https://www.academia.edu/31913298/Apocalyptic_of_Daniel_and_Revelation.

er dealt with before. But it actually uncovered many long-term issues that just bubbled to the surface where we could clearly see them.

> The pandemic didn't just create new hardships for impoverished communities, it revealed deficits that were already there—that have always been there.

And the same is true around the world. The pandemic didn't just create new hardships for impoverished communities, *it revealed deficits that were already there*—that have always been there. I saw this firsthand in the remote hills of Guatemala, where stable food supplies and clean water are already scarce.

As the pandemic spread, Guatemalans literally began raising white flags, signaling to the world that they were completely out of food. It was an acknowledgment of great distress and desperation. A universal sign of surrender, of collapse, of giving up.

Being in a place like Guatemala in the midst of a global catastrophe made all the other partisan debates (like those we were having in the U.S. at the time) seem small and irrelevant. Here, people were *scared*. Families living in extreme poverty are often not in the best health; on top of that, they lack access to medical care. They knew full well that if they got sick with something like COVID-19, it would most likely be a death sentence.

While I was there, Guatemala was in the middle of a lockdown called "Thirty Days of Calamity" because of the rise in cases. I visited one remote mountain village where nine teachers in their small school had tragically passed away from the disease.

It was in a similar village that little Jose was found. He was severely malnourished and only weighed about twenty-seven pounds. At 4 years old, he should have been closer to forty pounds. He had suffered with diarrhea for a month and was dehydrated, his stomach distended from the devastating effects of malnutrition and likely parasites.

Around the world, food insecurities that left people hungry before the pandemic only got worse after it hit. People were—and still are—starving. With hospitals overrun and oxygen in short supply, thousands were dying from COVID-19 at the time. In places like Guatemala, malnutrition soared. The United Nations predicted famines of biblical proportion around the world.[8]

And every single day, things just kept getting worse.

A few months later, we woke up to the news of a deadly earthquake in Haiti. Shortly after that, the Taliban captured the city of Kabul, sending hundreds of thousands fleeing for their lives. Meanwhile, political instability and racial divides raged in our own country. A massive hurricane swept through the Gulf of Mexico. The Russian invasion of Ukraine began. Another mass shooting stole the lives of innocent schoolchildren in Texas. *And then, and then, and then.* And it hasn't stopped. During those days it felt like the whole world was on fire in every sense of the word. It still does.

---

8 "As Famines of 'Biblical Proportion' Loom, Security Council Urged to 'Act Fast.'" 2020. UN News. April 21, 2020. https://news.un.org/en/story/2020/04/1062272

As global tragedies continue to unfold, many of us have the common refrain stuck in our heads on loop: *None of this is normal. This is not how things ought to be.*

Remember, the apocalypse isn't the end of the world—it's an unveiling— an opportunity to see what the world is really like, what we are really like. The apocalypse offers something better

But I believe it is precisely in these times that we need to be reminded that a truer vision of the world has already been given to us.

than a prediction of the future: *it offers us truth in the present.* It isn't the last line; it's the invitation to see the world as it really is—messy, heartbreaking, and yet somehow beautiful, somehow worth saving.

"I have told you these things, so that in me you may have peace. In this world you will have trouble. But take heart! I have overcome the world." Jesus spoke these words to His disciples to comfort them in a time of immense uncertainty—in times like today when we're tempted to believe that suffering is the only truth.

But I believe it is precisely in these times that we need to be reminded that a truer vision of the world has already been given to us. "The kingdom of heaven has come near." It isn't some distant dream. It's *here.* It's *now.* And it is already at work restoring every part of the world to God's original idea of wholeness. The desperate places. The persecuted places. Even in the streets of war-torn Syria.

PLEASE TAKE MY KIDS!

Mahdi's desperate plea crackled over the poor reception of the phone line. And our partner in Jordan thought he must have heard Mahdi incorrectly. But he repeated, "Please take my kids." He could no longer feed them.

The Syrian father lost his job during the pandemic and was no longer able to pay his rent or feed his family. He was already living an impossible life as a refugee in a land that was not his own, doing his best to support his family. And then the pandemic hit, and things only became worse. The loss of his job was the last straw. Facing homelessness and the thought of watching his children starve right before his eyes, Mahdi made an impossible choice.

Out of desperation he told our partner, "My wife and I can starve, but I want my children to live." He went on to say, "We don't want to be rich; we just want to have food to eat, to feed our kids, no more."

> If the gospel isn't good news for them, it isn't good news at all.

I don't know about you, but during the pandemic and lockdown, I wanted a lot more. I wanted to go out with my friends, and I wanted kids back in school. I wanted to go out to restaurants with no restrictions, host parties, have church at full capacity, travel internationally, and so much more. I wanted more. And there is nothing wrong with that necessarily—as long as we don't forget there are people around the world who simply want their kids to survive.

Through our work and our incredible partners, Mahdi was able to not only keep his children, but also to provide for them as well.

The world is full of people made in the image of God who have hopes and dreams too. Fathers like Mahdi who dream of a life beyond war for their children. Mothers in Guatemala who just want their kids to be happy and healthy. Children like Jose who, with access to basic resources, would flourish like our own children.

If the gospel isn't good news for them, *it isn't good news at all.*

The gospel must be good news for *the world.*

Scan the QR code for photos, videos, and more details about the stories from around the world shared in this chapter.

CHAPTER SEVEN / THE FREEDOM OF BOTH

NOW YOU KNOW

"You may choose to look the other way, but you can never say again that you did not know." Those words from William Wilberforce haunt me. Because now, I know.[1]

I had heard the stories. But when I finally stepped foot into that darkness for the first time, it was gut-wrenching. To bear witness to women being treated like animals—with no regard for their lives or well-being—was more than I could handle.

But the moment that broke me was when I went inside a dance bar in the heart of the red-light district in Bangkok. There, even the bars have different levels of depravity . . . and I was about to see the worst.

I don't say any of this to be exploitive or to get a reaction; I'm simply telling the truth. There are honestly no words to fully de-

---

1 "A Quote by William Wilberforce," Goodreads, accessed June 12, 2023,
https://www.goodreads.com/quotes/61653-you-may-choose-to-look-the-other-way-but-you.

scribe what I experienced there. What I saw out in the open on the streets did not prepare me for what was happening behind closed doors. What shocked me most was not the graphic nature of the women and girls dancing, but rather the interactions between them and their customers.

> ... while they were just numbers, they might as well have read: worthless, broken, unloved, slave, captive.

Each dancer was *numbered*—marked by a small circle of paper pinned to the few threads she was wearing. Numbers that might as well have been branded right into their skin. Marked and tagged like cattle. Men need only call out the number they wanted as if these human beings were being sold to the highest bidder.

Pick a number—15, 27, 195—any number. And while they were just numbers, they might as well have read: *worthless, broken, unloved, slave, captive.* Their empty eyes said it all.

We estimated there were over 200 girls in that bar alone. The bar owner just kept rotating them out on stage for the pleasure of the audience. It was degrading, disgusting, and completely infuriating. I was surrounded by men, many of whom were American, who had no shame in what they were doing.

This sickening practice all started with the Vietnam War. Soldiers on R&R came to Thailand, and people quickly realized there was money to be made. Fast forward fifty years, and now you have a booming industry with millions of men coming to

Thailand every year for sex. And before you convince yourself these are seedy-looking men, let me tell you they look just like your next-door neighbor or someone from your church.

It was all I could do to fight back the tears. I had stayed strong for days listening to so many stories, but this—this was too much. I finally made it out of the bar and into our waiting van and lost it. I sobbed and raged at the same time. Looking back now, it reminds me of that moment in the book, *The Green Mile*, where one of the main characters breathes in everyone's hurt and pain and suffering. I had breathed in too much evil, too much pain, and it had nowhere else to go anymore.

> **He often gives us way more than we can ever handle on our own.**

These powerful lines from the book describe the feeling with painful accuracy:

I'm rightly tired of the pain I hear and feel. It feels like pieces of glass in my head. I'm tired of all the times I've wanted to help and couldn't. I'm tired of being in the dark. Mostly it's the pain. There's too much. If I could end it, I would. But I can't.[2]

We have all heard the sentiment that God never gives us more than we can handle. I used to live by that. But I don't believe that anymore. I believe that God often does just that: He often gives us way more than we can ever handle on our own.

Our Thailand partner was sitting by me, patiently waiting for me to regain my composure. She does this day in and day out. She goes into the bars regularly and talks to the girls. She has seen it all.

---

2 King, Stephen. The Green Mile. Gollancz, 2008.

I asked her, "How do you do this every day? *How do you do it?*"

Her reply was a simple question: "If we don't go, who will?"

THE FRONT ROW

We could spend an entire book on the issues facing women around the world, especially those living in extreme poverty. But instead, I just want to give you a snapshot:

> If we don't go,
> who will?

- Globally, 650 million women and girls were married before the age of 18,[3] and at least 200 million women and girls in thirty countries have undergone female genital mutilation (FGM).[4]

- In eighteen countries, husbands can legally prevent their wives from working; in thirty-nine countries, daughters and sons do not have equal inheritance rights; and forty-nine countries lack laws protecting women from domestic violence.[5]

- One in ten females aged 15 to 49 has experienced physical and/or sexual violence by an intimate partner within the past twelve months.[6]

3 "Fast Facts: 10 Facts Illustrating Why We Must #Endchildmarriage," UNICEF, accessed May 5, 2023, https://www.unicef.org/eca/press-releases/fast-facts-10-facts-illustrating-why-we-must-endchildmarriage#:~:text=Worldwide%2C%20an%20estimated%20650%20million,at%2012%20million%20per%20yea

4 "Female Genital Mutilation (FGM) Statistics," UNICEF DATA, April 25, 2023, https://data.unicef.org/topic/child-protection/female-genital-mutilation/

5 Person, "In 18 Nations, Women Cannot Get a Job without Their Husband's Permission," The Wall Street Journal (Dow Jones & Company, September 9, 2015), https://www.wsj.com/articles/BL-REB-34010

6 23 August 2022, "In Focus: Sustainable Development Goal 5," UN Women – Headquarters, August 23, 2022, https://www.unwomen.org/en/news-stories/in-focus/2022/08/in-focus-sustainable-development-goal-5

- While women have made important inroads into political offices across the world, their representation in national parliaments at 23.7 percent is still far from parity.[7]
- At the current pace, it will take another forty years for men and women to be equally represented in national political leadership.[8]

I could also tell you how the search for clean water robs girls of an education around the world and how gender-based violence kills and incapacitates more women of reproductive age than cancer, malaria, and car accidents combined.[9]

Many of these issues are very different from the issues we face as women here in the U.S. and in most developed nations. We have our fair share of concerns including gender inequalities in the workplace, unequal pay, lack of access to affordable childcare, and more. We may still have a long way to go, but we also have seen incredible improvements and achievements.

But think about this for a moment: of the 8 billion people alive today, 3.92 billion are women. The population of women in the U.S. is 167 million.[10] When compared globally, that's a little more than 4 percent of the total global population of women. 4 percent!

Pretend for a moment that you are at a Broadway show in a decent-sized theater. It has a main level, a mezzanine, a lower

7 SDG 5—Gender Equality," AI for Good Foundation, October 12, 2022, https://ai4good.org/blog/sdg-5-gender-equality

8 "Gender Equality and Women's Empowerment," United Nations (United Nations), accessed May 5, 2023, https://www.un.org/sustainabledevelopment/gender-equality

9 "A Staggering One-in-Three Women, Experience Physical, Sexual Abuse | UN News," United Nations (United Nations), accessed May 5, 2023, https://news.un.org/en/story/2019/11/1052041

10 "Population, Female," World Bank Open Data, accessed May 5, 2023, https://data.worldbank.org/indicator/SP.POP.TOTL.FE.IN?end=2021&start=2021&view=map

balcony, and a second upper balcony. It even has those cool box seats on the side. Tonight, it's a packed house. Every seat is filled.

During a dramatic moment in the show, the entire audience jumps to its feet in roaring applause. But when the moment passes, everyone sits down, except for the front row. In a room full of thousands of people, the only ones standing are those in the front row.

> So when we talk about the state of women, about the issues facing women today, perhaps we should look at the whole theater and not just the front row.

That huge theater represents all the women in the world. And that front row represents women in the U.S., the 4 percent. So when we talk about the state of women, about the issues facing women today, perhaps we should look at the whole theater and not just the front row.

WHAT WOULD JESUS DO?

The red-light districts of Thailand are, in a word, overwhelming. The streets are buzzing with people. Music blares. And girls are being sold everywhere you turn. Just steps from my hotel was a large sign proudly displaying the words, "The World's Largest Adult Playground." It was in this chaos that I sat at a bar and met a young woman named Om. She had been working in the sex industry for two years.

You must understand that in Thailand, it is a woman's responsibility to provide financially for her family. So young girls from rural areas living in extreme poverty come to the big city looking for work. They get there, only to realize they have no education, no skills, and no qualifications to find a job that supports them, let alone their families back home. The bars offer them a "safe" place to sleep. They may start off as a cashier, but before long, one thing leads to another, and they end up trapped in the sex industry. They have made a choice they never thought they would make. A choice countless women make because they have no other choices.

I was surprised to learn that Om was only a few years younger than I am, and that we both have a son the same age. For a brief moment, I could relate to her. We have so much in common, yet our lives are worlds apart. We both love our sons and want to provide for them. But I have many choices on how to do that, with all the support I need and more. She has few to no options at all. I've realized that one of the greatest injustices of poverty is that it robs people of choices. And for Om, poverty had robbed her of any choice but the streets.

> A choice countless women make because they have no other choices.

I found myself overcome with the unfairness of it all—this woman's innocence was swept away in an instant, and she had no way out simply because she was poor. Simply because she had no education. Simply because she lived in an area of the world that was overcome with poverty. It didn't sit well with me. It wasn't right. She deserved choices like the rest of us. She deserved dignity. She deserved freedom.

With all the issues facing our world today, and especially those living in poverty, why should we single out the issues facing women? Why should we care?

> And at a time when women were treated as second-class citizens with few rights, Jesus's attitude toward women defied all cultural norms.

Well, if you share my faith, we worship a Savior who went out of His way to associate with women who were scorned by society. Someone who allowed a sex worker to wash His feet with her tears and dry them with her hair.[11] Someone who defended the woman caught in adultery, ultimately saving her life from an angry crowd ready to stone her to death.[12] To the Pharisees, Jesus said, "I tell you the truth, the tax collectors and the prostitutes are entering the kingdom of God ahead of you."[13]

Jesus valued women. And at a time when women were treated as second-class citizens with few rights, Jesus's attitude toward women defied all cultural norms.

Think about it. Jesus talked to women directly in public over and over again at a time when this was not culturally acceptable. Women were with Him from His birth to His death. Jesus did not shame the woman at the well. Jesus defended the woman caught in adultery. Women were the first to see Jesus and testify to His resurrection. Jesus spoke to women, ministered alongside them, healed them, and respected them.

11 Luke 7:36-50 (NIV)
12 John 8: 1-11 (NLT)
13 Matthew 21:31 (NIV)

One article summarizes how revolutionary this was:

> *[I]n Biblical times, it was very common, and expected, for women to be treated as 'less than.' That's one reason that the miracles of Christ healing women, spending time, reaching out, sharing truth with them is so important, even today. And why it was significant that the first people recorded as praying for and praising Him before He was born, giving financially to His ministry, lingering at the foot of the cross in His final moments, visiting the empty tomb after His death, and being the first to see Him again after the Resurrection were all women. These women followed and loved him, from birth to the cross.*[14]

As a woman and a leader of a global nonprofit, I find writing about women can be tricky. Do I care just because I am a woman? Is my passion slanted because I can relate more to the issues facing women? Perhaps.

But I think we have the opportunity to think of "women's issues" in another way. In *Half the Sky*, Nick Kristof writes, "Sex trafficking and mass rape should no more be seen as women's issues than slavery was a black issue, or the Holocaust was a Jewish issue."[15]

I couldn't agree more. But I also think there is another reason why we should care. You see, if Jesus doesn't convince you, then let the data do its work. Because focused programs geared to help women are strategic, sustainable, and cost-effective—and in the humanitarian world, one of the best ways to effect change.

14 James Borland (ThD, "How Jesus Viewed and Valued Women," Crossway, March 8, 2017, https://www.crossway.org/articles/how-jesus-viewed-and-valued-women/

15 Nicholas D. Kristof, Half the Sky: Turning Oppression into Opportunity for Women Worldwide, (New York, NY: Knopf Doubleday Publishing Group, 2010).

When you change the life of a girl, a young woman, a mother, a wife, you change the family, the village, the community, the nation, and yes, even the world. Studies show that women reinvest up to 90 percent of their incomes back into their families.[16]

> When you change the life of a girl, a young woman, a mother, a wife, you change the family, the village, the community, the nation, and yes, even the world.

There is no question the biggest bang for the buck in development is girls' education. It's been said that "If you educate a man you simply educate an individual, but if you educate a woman, you educate a whole nation."[17]

A World Bank study found that every year of secondary school education is correlated with an 18 percent increase in a girl's future earning power because educating girls has a multiplier effect.[18] Educated women tend to be healthier, participate more in the formal labor market, earn more, give birth to fewer children, marry at a later age, and provide better health care and education to their children. Yet, of the world's 130 million out-of-school youth, 70 percent are girls.[19]

As I write this, Afghanistan has banned secondary and university-level education for girls, essentially setting women's rights back thirty years.

16 "10 Reasons Why Investing in Women and Girls Is so Important," Global Citizen, accessed May 5, 2023, https://www.globalcitizen.org/en/content/10-reasons-why-investing-in-women-and-girls-is-so/

17 USA/Africa Dialogue, no. 21: Bangura, the hero that Africa needs, accessed May 5, 2023, https://www.laits.utexas.edu/africa/ads/21.html

18 World Bank Group, "World Bank Group to Invest $2.5 Billion in Education Projects Benefiting Adolescent Girls," World Bank (World Bank Group, April 12, 2016), https://www.worldbank.org/en/news/press-release/2016/04/13/world-bank-group-to-invest-25-billion-in-education-projects-benefiting-adolescent-girls

19 "Why Girls?," The Girl Impact, November 22, 2019, http://thegirlimpact.org/why-girls/

After being shot by the Taliban in 2012 for continuing to fight for girls' rights to an education, activist Malala Yousafzai said, "Extremists have shown what frightens them most: a girl with a book."[20]

A lack of education for girls can be directly tied to poverty. But it can also be used as a weapon—a weapon of oppression and control to deny women the opportunities and the voice they deserve.

There is a long history of girls and women being overlooked. The nonprofit organization Girl Effect points out that "for millions of girls across the developing world, there are no systems to record their birth, their citizenship, or even their identity."[21]

Think about it: nothing—not even a piece of paper—to acknowledge they exist or that they matter. It reminds me of the day I met Lakshmi.

ENDING A 500-YEAR-OLD TRADITION

At 14 years old, Lakshmi was forced into the sex trade by her parents due to their extreme poverty. She lives in a remote region of South Asia in a community called the Banchara (also commonly referred to as the Banchada). In the caste system, the Banchara community belongs in the lowest tier. The people are extremely poor and lack economic and developmental opportunities. Their lifestyle and beliefs sound like rumors or dark

20 Yousafzai, Malala. (@Malala). "The extremists have shown what frightens them most — a girl with a book." Twitter, Aug. 3, 2018, 10:29 a.m. https://twitter.com/Malala/status/1025388223810494466

21 The girl effect—education for girls—mother and child health and education trust, accessed May 5, 2023, https://educationforgirls.org/the-girl-effect.htm

secrets, but they live them openly for all to see and no one to stop. It is a nightmare they embrace, just to survive.

They have a tradition in place they call *Nari Mata*. For the past 500 years, they have been using prostitution as their primary source of income. The firstborn daughter of nearly every family is expected to enter into prostitution around the age of 12. What makes this even more shocking is that the parents and brothers initiate this, and the entire community lives off the earnings. But what started as a tradition affecting the eldest daughter now affects almost all the girls in this community.

It is a nightmare they embrace, just to survive.

Ten years after she was forced into sex work, Lakshmi has three children by one of her customers. She thought that customer would marry her; but of course, he did not. This work is the only way to take care of her children since she has no other skills. When I asked what the future holds for her daughter, I was shocked to hear her respond that, unless something changes, she will also send her daughter into the sex trade. A death sentence—spiritually, physically, and emotionally—for her own child. If she survives this lifestyle, Lakshmi will age out of the industry at 35 and most likely be sick the rest of her life.

Lakshmi deserves the right to choose a better life for both her and her daughter. But how can she when she has no feasible alternatives? When, for half a century, nearly every woman she's ever known has succumbed to this torture, just to keep her children alive?

Part of our work in the Banchara community is to provide women like Lakshmi with another choice. Deep in the heart of the community sits a beautiful building with rows of bunk beds where young girls who have been delivered from the sex trade have found a safe place to learn and grow. Here, they are educated and taught that they are valued. They learn about a God who loves them just as they are and who has a much better plan for their lives. In this safe environment, they are able to choose a life they never thought possible.

And here is the incredible thing: when you help just one girl, you end this vicious cycle for generations to come. That means Lakshmi's daughter will not go into this work, but neither will her daughter or her daughter's daughter. And that is how you begin to change the culture from the inside out.

> And here is the incredible thing: when you help just one girl, you end this vicious cycle for generations to come.

One of the experiences that impacted me the most was my visit to a Banchara village called Ponpour. It was here that the reality of the dowry system hit home. You see, not only is it the responsibility of the women—the daughters—to provide financially for their families, but they must also help their brothers pay dowries to the families of their future wives. A dowry can range anywhere from $5 to $20,000. You then add in corrupt money lenders who exploit the situation, leaving these young girls to work for the rest of their lives so their brothers can marry. And some of them have multiple brothers. It was infuriating.

It was in this village that I met an 18-year-old girl named Mayra. She began working in the industry at age 12. She has four brothers. Four dowries. It will take her forty years to pay off the dowries for her brothers to get married.

She told me she is regularly abused and mistreated, and that it is just expected. Then she said that if she had a way out, she would take it. She was longing for the freedom to break this vicious cycle.

And yet, as we were standing there talking, I was shocked to see customers gathering in the background just waiting for her. This was her everyday reality, surrounded by darkness that was about to swallow her whole.

I think I would have left feeling devastated and hopeless if not for one thing: right behind us, a new church building was being constructed in the village. And not just any church, but the first church in the entire Banchara community of 100,000 people—the very first church for this unreached people group.

A couple years ago, World Help was able to provide clean water for this community. People were getting sick and dying from the effects of drinking contaminated water. When we provided that well, we won the trust of the community. It was a simple need to meet, and it proved we cared about their lives here on earth now, not just where they would spend eternity. And that approach changed everything.

That clean water led to pastors visiting this community, helping reach even more girls, and eventually a new church building. This structure will not only be a place of worship, but also a place to gather, a community outreach center, and a hub for education, transforming the village from the inside out.

That is how you change a 500-year-old tradition. That is how you invade such darkness that is so deeply embedded within a culture. With freedom. Physical freedom for women trapped in the bondage of this work, and spiritual freedom to become all God wants them to be. You change it with both.

Here again is the magic of "both" and the freedom that is made possible as a result.

Here again is the magic of "both" and the freedom that is made possible as a result. Only holistic change can bring about true transformation. We have to make a physical and spiritual investment before freedom is possible.

If clean water is nearby, girls no longer have to spend their days fetching it and missing out on school. And if a girl can go to school, that means she can learn a trade that does not involve selling her body. And when she provides for her family, the economy of the community begins to change. There's no longer an excuse to force girls and women into becoming sex workers against their will. The barriers are both physical and spiritual, so the transformation must be both too. Freedom is only possible through both.

A FUTURE FOR ALL WOMEN

You know, I like to think of myself as a strong, powerful

woman. And I could not be more supportive of women's rights both around the world and right here at home. I want every little girl to dream the dreams she was meant to dream and to believe she can do and accomplish anything.

We've been fortunate in the West to have courageous women use their platforms to confront sexual abuse. But the women from the Banchara community and Thailand's red-light districts have few, if any, options to fight back and few who will listen or care. These women have been saying "Me too," "Times up," and "Enough," in some cases for hundreds of years. It's time somebody listens to them.

Women make up half the human race. And in this country, we represent only a small part of it—the front row. So, I can't help but wonder how much work could be done and how much good could be accomplished if we focused on the global issues facing women today. If we truly cared about the common good of our sisters around the globe, perhaps we would use our freedom a bit differently.

Our freedom as women is an issue that crosses all barriers, borders, and racial lines. We don't have everything in common, but that doesn't mean we can't fight for each other. We can fight

Women who are free, free other women.

for someone else's daughter, someone else's mother, someone else's family. Women who are free, free other women.

I know this is not the experience of all, but I am the daughter of a man who raised me believing I could do anything I put my mind to. He has literally given me the opportunities and platform to do what I do today. I am the wife of a man who not only loves me, but also has always supported my dreams. And I am the proud mom of two adult sons whom I hope I have raised to treat women with the respect and dignity they deserve. In no way do I want the fighting for the flourishing of mothers and daughters to diminish the value and importance of fathers and sons. I don't want their freedom reduced to give women more.

> By prioritizing women, we are loving BOTH in the most effective and sustainable way possible.

No, I'm saying there is no such thing as partial liberation. By prioritizing women, we are loving BOTH in the most effective and sustainable way possible.

A woman in rural Uganda who now has access to clean water no longer has to spend hours every day fetching water. She now has the time to learn a trade or start a business to provide for her family. And her children are less likely to die from waterborne illnesses.

Brave women in China and Cuba now have the resources and help they need to live out their faith. They pursue their calling as church planters in some of the most hard-to-reach places, leading hundreds to Christ.

A young woman in Thailand has another option besides the streets and bars of the sex trade. With a safe place to live and an education, she can, for the first time, choose a life she really dreams of—not one forced upon her. And by doing so, she breaks the cycle for her daughters and granddaughters.

Women embody the beauty of both.

 Scan the QR code for photos, videos, and more details about the stories from around the world shared in this chapter.

CHAPTER EIGHT / THE VISION OF BOTH

LOOK UP

My son Riley attended college in Nashville, Tennessee. He is a musician, so naturally it was a perfect spot for him and a great place to drop by for a visit.

On one particular trip I was helping him move into a new apartment. After a long day of hauling furniture, we decided to take a break and go grab a bite to eat. He suggested we head to his favorite sushi place downtown, and so we did—without bothering to make a reservation. It was a Tuesday night in the summer. What could go wrong?

Needless to say, it was definitely a bad move. The restaurant was slammed with summer tourists, and there were no open tables when we arrived. Reluctantly, we decided to stick out the wait. Riley and I plopped ourselves down on a bench in the reception area and distractedly scrolled through our phones to pass the time.

I almost didn't notice the woman walking out of the restroom area and back into the dining room. And, at first, I didn't even bother looking all the way up. From the waist down, I saw what's become a stereotypical look of Nashville tourists—boots, jeans, fringe, and rhinestones as if

> ... how often in life do we see half-truths and mistake them for the whole truth?

they're all on their way to an actual rodeo. My first thought was something ungenerous like, *"Ahh, look at her. She's trying so hard."*

But right before she passed by, I happened to look up from my phone. And then I realized . . . it was Reba. *Reba McIntire.* The real, honest-to-goodness Reba McIntire. The Queen of Country. The legend. *Fancy herself!*

She looked right at us and smiled as she walked by in all her glory, just like you would imagine. It was a moment, for me at least. And if anyone has the right to dress however she wants, it's Reba freaking McIntire!

I was so excited that I hit my son with my elbow and blurted out, "Look! That's Reba!" To which he replied, "Who's Reba?"

Seriously?

I still don't know if my inner '90s country fan can forgive him for that. But here's my point: how often in life do we see half-truths and mistake them for the whole truth?

How often do we only open our eyes part of the way or look up enough to see part of the story and miss the whole?

The truth is, we miss so much when we're only looking halfway up. We miss so much about people when we see them only as souls to be saved. We miss so much about people when we see them only as bodies to feed and clothe.

Our actions remain limited—incomplete at best and harmful at worst—when our vision of people is skewed. God made people with bodies and souls on purpose. And in order to serve them, we need to serve both.

I've been thinking about the connection between love and looking up. The Gospel of Matthew describes the relationship vividly in the ministry of Jesus. It says: "Then Jesus made a circuit of all the towns and villages. He taught in their meeting places, reported kingdom news, and healed their diseased bodies, healed their bruised and hurt lives. When he looked out over the crowds, his heart broke."[1]

**Love looks up.
Love sees.**

When He looked, His heart broke.

Love looks up. Love sees. And when we take the time to look up, we can see what God sees: the invisible, the neglected, the desperate, the lonely.

I witnessed one of the best examples of this during an eye-opening trip to Honduras.

1 Matthew 9:35-36 (MSG)

WHAT DO YOU SEE?

It was foreboding. Apocalyptic. An assault on all the senses. Completely and utterly overwhelming. Those are the best words I have to describe this scene.

You could see it from far away and smell it from an even farther distance. It is the largest trash dump in all of Honduras, and it sits right outside the capital city.

I stopped and stared in disbelief at the columns of rising smoke, at the mounds of trash as far as the eye could see, at the haunting image of birds circling overhead and people digging. People—men, women, and children—on their hands and knees, sifting through the stench and the refuse and the ruin with their bare hands. Needless to say, I had never been more grateful to be wearing a mask.

Even though I had witnessed similar scenes in other countries—countless families forced to live and work at dumpsites just to survive—not every dump is run by gangs who control the whole operation. Not every dump is this vast and ominous.

Hundreds of people come here to work every day, digging through the trash for things of value and eating any food they can find to fight off their hunger. They hand over what they find to the gang who then sells it and pays the families next to nothing; suffice it to say, there is no negotiation.

Honduras is a place where issues like extreme poverty, gang violence, lack of education and opportunities, and the highest femicide rate in the world—every sixteen hours a woman is murdered[2]—all collide to make it an extremely dangerous and hopeless place to live. And yet, it's often the hopeless places, the dark places, where our vision becomes even clearer.

> And yet, it's often the hopeless places, the dark places, where our vision becomes even clearer.

I met a beautiful and hilarious woman named Daisy with a personality you just can't resist. I'm not sure it translated well, but I told her we would call her "sassy" back home, and that if I could just speak Spanish, I knew we would be fast friends. I loved meeting Daisy.

But after meeting her and many other moms in Honduras, I was left with this nagging thought: *All moms sacrifice for their kids, but some seem to sacrifice it all.* Daisy is one of those moms.

Daisy works in the dump during the day to support her family. Earlier, our partners had told me a tragic story of a little boy who was killed in the dump when the driver of one of the garbage trucks did not see him.

Well, it is one thing to hear that horrific story. It is quite another to stand in the home of the mother who lost that son and see his picture hanging on the wall. You see, that mom is Daisy.

Daisy's first husband died when he was electrocuted in a freak accident. She moved to the capital for a better life, but that better life meant working in the dump to survive.

2 teleSUR / kb-OA-gp, "In Honduras, 1 Woman Killed Every 16 Hours," News | teleSUR English (teleSUR, November 18, 2015), https://www.telesurenglish.net/news/In-Honduras-1-Woman-Killed-Every-16-Hours-20151118-0019.html

Then she met her second husband, who also later died after eating something out of the dump that made him very sick. Can you even imagine?

Daisy is now left alone with her five children. They live in an area of extreme poverty completely run by the gangs. It is a dangerous community that you just don't walk into on your own. We had to be accompanied by a police escort just to visit her home.

Yet somehow Daisy has created a happy home and one where she values her children's education. She told us her greatest wish is that her kids can focus on their education and a better life.

> **When we see the world not with mere pity, but also with compassion, our love takes action.**

Daisy's dream for her children is becoming a reality because perfectly positioned in this community, and right across the street from that vast dump, sits a beacon of light and hope. A place where the children can escape this grueling work and instead get an education, nutritious food, medical care, clean clothing, and a bath. Here they are introduced to a God who loves them and has a future for them.

Daisy's son Wilson wants to be a police officer; Dolce, Isis, and Dario want to be doctors; and Michael wants to be a fireman.

Daisy still works in the dump. It's a sacrifice she makes every day for her family. But in all of this suffering, Daisy still has a reason to hope. Her children will have opportunities that she never had and a chance to reach their dreams. And by reaching their dreams, they will fulfill Daisy's dream as well.

The question is, do we have eyes to see people like Daisy as more than their circumstances? Do we only see a woman and her family stuck in a tragic cycle of poverty? Do we only see a soul to add to our heavenly club? Do we see possibilities? Do we see reality? Do we see despair? Do we see hope? Do we see *her*?

When we see the world not with mere pity, but also with compassion, our love takes action.

LIGHT CHANGES EVERYTHING

Readers, readers, everywhere. In my car, on my desk, beside my bed, in every drawer. For years I kept these glasses everywhere I was, thinking I just needed a little extra help when reading.

Eventually, I started to notice that my eyesight was getting worse, so I made an eye appointment to get a prescription. But instead of a new prescription, I walked out with a new diagnosis: glaucoma. I knew I wasn't getting any younger, but after that appointment, I felt really, really old.

The doctor informed me that I would need a minor surgery in about a year to help relieve the pressure building up in my eyes. And then he said, "You know, if you were going to Africa or something, I would be worried, but as long as you are staying around here, you should be fine."

I couldn't help but chuckle before saying, "Well, that might be a problem." Not only do I visit Africa more often than the average person due to the nature of my work, but I'm also often in remote locations far from reliable cell service or a clean water source—let alone specialized emergency medical care.

Long story short, I had that surgery earlier than expected. For a couple years, all my appointments centered around making sure my glaucoma was in check. But, in the meantime, my overall eyesight was still awful, and I spent most of my time cycling through my little collection of reading glasses.

So again, I broke down and went to the doctor just to get a new prescription. I decided I was tired of glasses. I wanted contacts. It's no exaggeration to say that when the doctor put those contacts in my eyes for the first time, I could not believe it. I didn't realize how bad my vision had become. I just thought I needed help reading, but I actually needed help seeing! When I opened my eyes with those new contacts, everything was clear and crisp, and the whole world was new.

Light changes everything.

I was like a little kid who had been given the best present ever. A brighter, more vibrant world opened up for me. I was so excited until I looked in the mirror next to me and realized I could see every little fine line and wrinkle that I had not seen clearly in years.

As my doctor was explaining all the things I needed to know as someone new to wearing contacts, he told me that even with the contacts it would still be much easier to read with good lighting. And then he casually said, "Light changes everything."

Light changes everything. That stuck with me.

Maybe you have heard of light pollution. It's the artificial light that contaminates our night sky, limiting our view of the stars. That's why the stars are clearer and brighter the farther away you go from all the artificial lights. Because of all the city lights, it's hard to clearly see the beauty and vividness of the stars lighting up the sky. Typically, if you want to look through a telescope to see celestial objects in deep space, you have to go somewhere that's pitch black. Only then can you see the night sky as it truly is—littered with brilliant stars and planets.

We are not lost in the darkness; we are lost in the light.

There are so many places around the world where I have felt true darkness, and even almost got lost in it. In contrast, what I have realized is that here at home we live in a bright world—a blindingly, bright world. We are not lost in the darkness; we are lost in the light.

This artificial light can distract us from the true needs that exist. Distractions of our comfortable lives: Netflix binging, vacations, shopping, and overall busyness of our day-to-day schedules. If we aren't leaving room in our lives to see the darkness, then we can't see people who are in desperate need. And when we are "lost in light," we can't reach into the darkest places of our world with the light of hope.

I have decided this: I would much rather stay in the darkness than live in a place that is so bright I can't even see real darkness.

There's a familiar verse found at the beginning of the Gospel of John. You probably know it. I have heard it my whole life. But recently, I started to read this verse and understand it in an entirely new way.

John 1:5 tells us that "the light shines in the darkness and the darkness has not overcome it."[3]

The light can't shine in the darkness unless it is in the darkness.

There is an important word in this verse that somehow I had missed every other time I read it. It's a little two-letter word: *in*. What it tells us is that the light shines *in* the darkness.

Here is what I realized. The light can't shine in the darkness unless it is *in the darkness*. You have to be inside of the darkness itself in order to witness the light. When you are willing to step out of the light into that complete darkness, then—and only then—do you see God's redemptive plan and the story He is writing across the sky. Only then can you see the glimmers of hope. The darkness is not a thing to run from; it is the home of the stars. It is the place where hope is born.

Once you step out of the light, out of all the comfort and safety, you can begin to see clearly—perhaps for the very first time. Sometimes, those who need you most are just outside the light.

Finding the courage to enter into the darkness is the only way our light will truly shine. And if we truly want to join God in

3 John 15 (NIV)

His kingdom work, we have to embrace the darkness. Don't get lost in light. Get lost in the darkness.

Light changes everything if we are willing to see and willing to act.

SEE THE ONE

We walked for what seemed like an hour to reach a makeshift home in the middle of what is widely considered one of the worst slums in Uganda. Our team was led through narrow and steep alleys where you had to watch your every step and at the same time make sure your arm or head did not come too close to the ragged metal roofing or a live wire.

We stepped over trash, streams of water mixed with sewage, and animal waste. And while every step worried me, I watched with a mix of anxiety and amazement as barefooted children ran freely.

> Finding the courage to enter into the darkness is the only way our light will truly shine.

Even though I have seen extreme poverty around the world, there is something about this place that almost takes your breath away. Thousands live here in extremely close quarters. It is dangerous and desperate. And people—especially women and girls—must do desperate things to survive.

On one particular visit to Katwe, my driver explained the dark side of Uganda's worst slum at night. (Although I have to admit it doesn't exactly radiate hope during the day either.) He told me that "Jesus leaves Katwe at dark because He cannot look at the things that happen there."

But, Katwe was also Jerry's home.

Jerry's mom was a prostitute and his father, a complete stranger. Even as an infant, Jerry was left alone for hours without food, water, or protection. As a single mother, Jerry's mom had difficulty caring for him. She had little education and no stable way to provide for him. She sold herself on the streets, but even that did not make ends meet. Eventually out of complete desperation, his mother did the unthinkable. She left to look for money and never came home. Jerry was abandoned. He was only 2 years old.

Five days passed before anyone noticed that little Jerry was all alone. He was almost dead when they found him. In our partner's words, "Jerry needed a rescuer. He needed someone to rescue him. The baby was almost passing out. He was almost dead. He was like someone who is already in the grave."

Jerry was brought to our partner's Rescue Center where he received the immediate lifesaving help he needed. Loving house mothers provided him with nutritious food, a warm bed, and all the love that little boy could take. Day by day, he grew stronger. And eventually, he began to smile.

I call little Jerry "the rock star of Uganda." Maybe I should also start calling him the "king of Katwe." It's like he knows how much I love to share his rescue story. And what a rescue story it is.

Another partner shared these reflections on Jerry's rescue:

Rescuing someone . . . someone who has lost hope . . . someone who is going to die . . . someone who is lost completely and then giving that person hope is showing that person their destiny. We believe that Jerry has a destiny. When you look at him, he is a bright young boy. We believe he is a leader.

If the children get educated, if they can get skills, it can help them sustain their lives and also their family . . . they get skills and then they prosper, they excel. Maybe someday in the future they will help someone else. Like Jerry, we believe he is going to be somebody—a lawyer, a minister, doctor, the president.

I couldn't agree more.

Today, Jerry is not so little. As I am writing this, he is 12 years old and finishing elementary school. His future is bright. He will have the opportunity to dream whatever he wants for his life and be able to reach those dreams because of our partners' support. And maybe, just maybe, he will one day become president. I would not be surprised one bit.

But that little 2 year-old Jerry would never have been found unless someone was willing to go into the darkness of Katwe. Someone saw. Someone stopped. Someone rescued him.

> The moment of rescue is always right in front of us, if we choose to see.

Some rescues, like Jerry's, are dramatic. They are life-and-death moments. And some are simple everyday encounters. But the moment of rescue is always right in front of us, if we choose to see.

THE VISION TO SEE BOTH

A few years ago, I was in New York City for an event in the financial district. While I was there, I visited what has become an iconic statue. I had heard a friend share about it, and I just had to see it for myself. It is the life-sized figure of a fearless girl cast in bronze that sits right across the street from the stock exchange. Passersby will find her feet firmly planted on the ground, head up, her hands on hips, and her eyes staring down a giant bull in front of her. *Fearless.*

So, what do you do when you visit an iconic statue? Well, of course you get your picture taken standing in the same exact pose. Feet firmly planted, head up, hands on hips, staring down the bull. And you try to give that fierce, fearless look.

> I believe that when we stand firm, we can choose to not only fearlessly see the overwhelming problems of our time, but we can also choose to fearlessly see the overwhelming hope on the other side.

But as I got closer, I noticed something. Actually, the girl is not looking the bull in the eye, but rather staring right over his head. She is looking beyond the bull and clearly seeing what is on the other side.

Sometimes the world's problems seem to be like that bull. They are overwhelming and powerful—whether it is a refugee crisis, children dying from the effects of dirty water and malnutrition,

Christians being persecuted, women trapped in slavery, or millions suffering in extreme poverty.

South African Anglican bishop and theologian, Desmond Tutu, said that "hope is being able to see that there is light despite the darkness."[4] I believe that when we stand firm, we can choose to not only fearlessly see the overwhelming problems of our time, but we can also choose to fearlessly see the overwhelming hope on the other side.

We can fearlessly choose to see both.

---

4 Charlayne Hunter-Gault, "Remembering Desmond Tutu's Hope," The New Yorker (The New Yorker, December 27, 2021), https://www.newyorker.com/news/postscript/remembering-desmond-tutus-hope.

Scan the QR code for photos, videos, and more details about the stories from around the world shared in this chapter.

CHAPTER NINE / THE POWER OF BOTH

TRANSFORMATIVE HOPE

In the timeless children's picture book by Eric Carle, we meet a very hungry caterpillar. If you know the story or if you have read it to your children countless times, then you know how it goes. The very hungry caterpillar keeps eating day after day, never getting full. On day one, he eats one apple. On day two, he eats two pears. On day three, he eats three plums. You get the point. This goes on until after six days of eating all the things, he is no longer a small, hungry caterpillar—instead, he's a big, fat caterpillar. He then builds a small home around him where he "cocoons" himself away and gradually transforms into a beautiful butterfly.

Maslow's Hierarchy of Needs[1] teaches us the importance of humans having their basic needs met before they can truly transform. You could say that hunger for food and safety leads to hunger for belonging, knowledge, self-worth, and a connection to a higher power.

---

1 "Maslow's Hierarchy of Needs: What Is It?," WebMD (WebMD), accessed May 5, 2023, https://www.webmd.com/mental-health/what-is-maslow-hierarchy-of-needs

In the same way, true transformation is always preceded by hunger. Help is the catalyst for metamorphosis—essential to its very existence. But hope (in the cocoon) is a new birth. It's hope, in the end, that transforms us.

People in desperate situations can't be "fixed" with a little food, a dose of medicine, and an encouraging pat on the back. That's a nice thought, but it's simply not enough. True, lasting change only happens within long-term relationships built on trust—when the needs of an entire person (heart, mind, body, and soul) are met with the same care and attention. Try as we may to separate help and hope into two palatable categories with checklists, the power is in how interchangeable they are.

> ### It's hope, in the end, that transforms us.

Throughout the history of World Help, people have tried to pigeonhole us into neat little categories. What do you do to meet the physical needs of people? What do you do to meet the spiritual needs of people? When you provide water, do you also give a Bible? And if you give a Bible, do you also give a cup of cold water?

But I understand why. People of faith want to make sure their generous gifts are being used to further the gospel. They don't want to swing the pendulum too far toward social justice and neglect the spiritual. And justice seekers don't want to swing the pendulum too far toward preaching, Bibles, and tracts, while ignoring the needs of the body. But once again, what if we can actually do both?

The Gospels tell us the story of Jesus's life here on earth. We read how Jesus gave sight to a man who had been blind since birth. How He fed 5,000 with just two fish and five loaves of bread. How He healed the Roman officer's son without even seeing him. How He turned water into wine at a wedding celebration. And how He healed a woman of a bleeding disorder just by her touching the hem of His cloak.

So, what if I asked you the following questions and you had to answer specifically one or the other?

> ... while He did physically heal them, He also healed and changed their hearts.

Were these healings and miracles physical or spiritual? Was Jesus meeting physical needs or spiritual needs? Remember, you can't answer "both." It can only be one or the other. You have to choose.

My guess is you are thinking the same thing I am—this sounds ridiculous. Of course Jesus was meeting both at the same time. His work reached straight down to the depths of their souls. His love pierced through the deepest parts of their hearts. And while He did physically heal them, He also healed and changed their hearts.

As Jesus fed the hungry multitude, the disciples learned that when it comes to following Jesus, the impossible is possible.

The blind man who could see for the very first time realized his true blindness was in his heart and put his faith in Jesus.

And when Jesus healed the woman with bleeding, not only

was she healed of a physical condition that had plagued her for twelve years, but also her faith in a Savior was validated. As she trembled before Jesus, afraid she was going to be in trouble for touching His clothes, He instead gave her a blessing: "Go with peace in your heart and be free from your suffering" (Mark 5:34).[2]

So why is it so hard for us to believe His work can still do the same today? To believe that a cup of cold water in Jesus's name can be just as "spiritual" as handing someone a Bible?

Why is it so hard for us to believe that the physical and spiritual can be one and the same? That meeting the needs of the body has a spiritual impact. That the physical can be spiritual and that the spiritual can be physical. That help and hope can be BOTH.

> ... we should leave the people we encounter with peace in their heart and freedom from their suffering.

Now don't get me wrong. I am not Jesus. You are not Jesus. But we can be the hands and feet of Jesus to a hurting world. And my prayer for every encounter I have in my work—every refugee I meet fleeing war and conflict, every father struggling to feed his family, every woman desperate for freedom—is the same as the blessing Jesus gave to the woman.

And this should be the prayer of every person of faith. In order for earth to look a little more like heaven, we should leave the people we encounter with peace in their heart and freedom from their suffering.

I believe that help is both physical and spiritual. And hope is both physical and spiritual. Perhaps the difference lies in the timing. Help is immediate. Hope lies in the future.

Because, at the end of the day, help is hope, and hope is help. They are a singular message of good news, and their power lies in what they are able to transform together.

When help and hope serve one another, they have power over fear. When help and hope are together, they inspire a greater imagination for the future. When help and hope are practiced together in harmony, they look—to the world—like miracles. The power of both is, by nature, utterly transformative.

> ... at the end of the day, help is hope, and hope is help.

HOPE IS A LONG GAME

High above the Kathmandu valley sits Swayambhunath, an ancient religious temple that is said to be one of the most sacred among Buddhist pilgrimage sites.

After a winding drive up the mountain, followed by never-ending steps, you reach a huge dome-shaped shrine that is supposed to represent the entire world. And the eyes painted on it represent a person awakening to wisdom and compassion.

But what you really need to know about this place is that it is commonly called "The Monkey Temple." Why, you ask? Well, because there are "holy" monkeys there . . . and I mean everywhere.

I had been warned not to have any loose items or my phone in my back pocket because the monkeys will steal them. *What?* I was told they are very naughty monkeys. *Fabulous, can't wait. Let me just check and see if my rabies vaccination is up to date.*

As we pulled up to the temple, my colleague said, "Oh, make sure you don't show them your teeth. That's a sign of aggression." *Sure, okay. Good to know.*

From the moment you get out of the car and before you even start up the steep steps, you see them. Above you, beside you, and in front of you. And let's just say, they are not shy.

The babies are super cute, but that doesn't make up for the adults that are literally tearing each other apart fighting in front of you.

But what my colleague failed to mention is that there were also countless stray dogs—one of my worst fears in foreign countries. And there were pigeons. So many pigeons. It was not my favorite trifecta. Just add some snakes, and I would have been done.

So, while most visitors around me were coming there as a peaceful experience on their religious pilgrimage, I was on high alert.

And in the middle of all that chaos, my team thought it would be a great time to sit down and film some of my thoughts on our work in Nepal. *Great. Yes. This is the place. Definitely right here. I will surely be able to focus with all of these monkeys flying over my head. No problem.*

But even with all the commotion around me, when I did sit down, I tried to process what I had learned from my time in Nepal. And here is what I realized.

This is a place where we have been working for the past twenty-five years. We have child sponsorship programs, church-planting initiatives, Bible distribution, clean water projects, and much more. It's a beautiful place with beautiful people. But it's also a place where extreme poverty threatens lives and futures—but where hope is being kindled each day by our partners.

And although we did respond and help rebuild after the devastating 2015 earthquake, our daily presence there isn't because of a massive refugee crisis or humanitarian disaster. It isn't big or flashy or "urgent" in terms of being newsworthy. But it's a crisis all the same. The slow drip of poverty is what silently steals away the lives of the most vulnerable in our world every day.

But you know what? Hope is also a slow drip. It's something that seems small and insignificant by itself, but after years and decades, it transforms into a rushing stream. Hope is a day-by-day investment in a future we can't see yet.

I saw the future in Nepal that my dad and so many World Help supporters must have imagined decades ago. I saw it in the faces of individuals who were in our programs as children and who now have their own businesses and families. I saw it in our sponsorship programs, which help lift entire families out of poverty. I saw it in packed church buildings that didn't exist a few years ago.

I've been so conditioned to the crises of our world. The refugee crisis, a war in Ukraine, a global pandemic, famine—even the ongoing issue of trafficking has a feel of urgency to it.

But I recognized that extreme poverty (both spiritual and physical) is a crisis all on its own, although one that feels very different. The truth is, the repercussions of that everyday poverty reach farther than any single humanitarian disaster that may steal our attention.

And once again, the answer does not lie in one or the other. No, the answer is found in both.

We don't quit responding to the crises caused by war and earthquakes; but with the same passion and urgency, we also continue to fight those hidden battles that rarely make the news.

You can't fight spiritual and physical poverty with a crisis response. Fighting poverty is a long game, not a short one. Ending the vicious cycle of poverty takes commitment year after year after year. It takes investing in a life. It takes a relationship, trust, and empowerment. It takes the vision to see that true transformation takes time.

And after so many years in Nepal, we are reaping the rewards of that long-term investment. An investment that continues month after month and year after year. An investment that gives so many children a safe place to live and nutritious food to eat. An investment that allows them to have an education and pursue their dreams. An investment that allows them to find a job. An investment that empowers them to choose a different way of life and break the cycle of poverty.

I could tell you story after story of the lives that are being changed because of our work on the ground. I listened as our partner shared the story of Arul, a little girl I had watched smile and dance with the other children. She was so happy, but I had no idea of her tragic story.

Arul's father had a very difficult childhood. He lost his leg as a boy when his mother threw him and herself on the train tracks out of sheer desperation. She simply couldn't afford to care for him. But Arul's father survived and went on to have a family of his own and become a pastor. The hardships, however, continued. He and Arul's mother were often persecuted and beaten for their faith.

Recently he was abused so severely that he needed to go to the hospital. But before he checked himself in, he dropped Arul off with our partner where he knew she would be safe. He was admitted to the hospital for his injuries but caught COVID-19 and tragically passed away, never returning for little Arul. Left without her husband and with no way to adequately provide, Arul's mother came to the heartbreaking realization that she could no longer care for her daughter. In an instant, Arul's life changed forever.

My heart just broke for this little girl. But, as hard as that story was to hear, I couldn't help but notice how she was thriving. How she was surrounded by people who loved her. How she had a safe place to live and call home. How she was sponsored and was receiving an education. How she had hope for the future and the opportunity to reach her dreams. And how the vicious cycle of poverty could once and for all end with her.

You see, the investments we have made—and are making—are literally paying off.

There's Rashmi, who grew up in our sponsorship program and is now one of the top students in Nepal. Timothy, who is now a pastor. Vijay, who has dedicated his life to helping the people of his country. And Deepesh, who is now all grown up and owns a trucking business from which we rented our vehicle for the week. And when we tried to pay, he would not let us. He said World Help had done so much for him, and he would not take our money.

I'm here to tell you that this model works. That help and hope work. That long-term commitment to trusted partners and the people they serve—works. And it yields incredible results.

REBELLIOUS HOPE

She walked onto that global stage and, in just a matter of minutes, captured the judges' hearts and absolutely blew them away with her talent. Her performance prompted the much-coveted golden buzzer. As the gold streamers rained down, she was instantly inducted into pop-culture history.

The incredible story of Nightbirde will continue to inspire for years to come. But it wasn't just her amazing performance on *America's Got Talent* that caught my attention. It wasn't even her unique and haunting voice. It was her story that captured my heart and the heart of the world.

She was in her early thirties and suffering from cancer. Without a miracle, her chances were slim. But you would have never known that. It was obvious she was a person of faith, and that is what resonated with people. Her unwavering hope, literally in the face of death, was absolutely inspiring.

Her simple yet relatable and hopeful song included lyrics like, "It's okay, it's okay, it's okay, it's okay / if you're lost, we're all a little lost, and it's all right."[3]

But what really got to me was an interview she gave. After her breakout performance and the world learning of her diagnosis, she was asked how she stays so positive despite her circumstances. She said she calls it "Rebellious Hope."

> ... not denying the present pain, but also not denying the future hope.

She defined that as not denying the present pain, but also not denying the future hope.

You may have heard of a similar thought in what is called the Stockdale Paradox, made famous by Jim Collins in his book, *Good to Great*. The paradox name refers to Admiral Jim Stockdale, who survived being a prisoner of war for more than seven years. "You must never confuse faith that you will prevail in the end—which you can never afford to lose—with the discipline to confront the most brutal facts of your current reality, whatever they might be,"[4] Stockdale said.

But back to Nightbirde. Here is what she said in that interview

---

3 Nightbirde, "It's Okay," original song performed on *America's Got Talent*, June 8, 2021.

4 "What the Stockdale Paradox Tells Us about Crisis Leadership," HBS Working Knowledge, August 17, 2020, https://hbswk.hbs.edu/item/what-the-stockdale-paradox-tells-us-about-crisis-leadership

that I just can't forget: "Don't you want to see what happens if you don't give up?"

Don't you want to see what happens if you don't give up? Wow. Yes, yes I do.

> ## Don't you want to see what happens if you don't give up?

Because I've decided I want to be known for my "rebellious hope." Hope that does not ignore the present pain of the world, but never believes that there is nothing we can do, that this is just the way it is. I never want to let go of that future hope of a new kingdom, a world redeemed.

I love how 2 Corinthians 4:16-18 sums it up:

> *So, we are not giving up. How could we! Even though on the outside it often looks like things are falling apart on us, on the inside, where God is making new life, not a day goes by without his unfolding grace. These hard times are small potatoes compared to the coming good times, the lavish celebration prepared for us. There's far more here than meets the eye. The things we see now are here today, gone tomorrow. But the things we can't see now will last forever.[5]*

I wish I could share an alternate ending for Nightbirde's story—one with a triumphant conclusion—an "I beat cancer" story. But I can't. Nightbirde passed away. But not before inspiring the world with her very own rebellious hope. She never gave up.

5 2 Corinthians 4:16-18 (MSG)

Never. And she continued spreading her message of hope until the end of her life. But her legacy lives on.

Her life and message make me want to ask so many questions:

What would happen if we didn't give up?

What would happen in our churches, organizations, and ministries?

What would happen in the lives of those we lead and serve?

What would happen in our families?

What would happen in underserved communities around the world?

What would happen in the midst of chaos, disaster, and death?

Don't you want to see what happens if you don't give up?
I do.

You see, help and hope require us to see the brutal reality of the world and its needs. And whether our investment is short-term or long-term, we need both help and hope to do each well. Help for today for a world on fire, and rebellious hope for a tomorrow that wants to see what happens when we refuse to give up.

Scan the QR code for photos, videos, and more details about the stories from around the world shared in this chapter.

CHAPTER TEN / BOTH IS WHAT WE DO

THE FIRE STATION

A couple of years ago, I arrived home one day to find I was locked out. We were temporarily living in a third-floor apartment, and there was just one way in and one way out. My teenage son was home but had accidentally turned the lock that was only accessible from the inside.

So, I began knocking on the door. No response. I knocked louder. Again, no response.

I called him from my cell phone. No answer. Over and over again, no answer. It's nearly impossible to get teenagers—or really kids of any age—to answer or respond to a text. But if *you* don't respond, you'll receive the equivalent of *MOM???* in all caps.

I was confused because I had just talked to him a few minutes before I got there. He had mentioned he was not feeling well and was going to lie down. *He's probably fine, Noel.*

For a few minutes, I was cool. But after ten minutes with no response, I started to worry. I called my husband who was hours away at the time, and he started calling our son too. Again, no response. I can't tell you how hard I pounded on that door! I even resorted to banging on my neighbors' door. Since apartments share walls, I thought maybe they could beat on my son's bedroom wall in case he had just fallen asleep; but of course, they were not home.

So, after about twenty minutes, I started to lose it. My mind went to worst-case scenarios. At the time, we were in the middle of a pandemic. He had not been feeling well . . . could something have happened? How could he not hear my knocking and calling? *Something must be wrong.* And my husband on the phone was not helping. He was worried too. Finally he said, "Noel, you need to go next door to the fire station and get them to help." (Yes, we lived next to a fire station, which made for noisy nights and interrupted Zoom calls).

But seriously? How embarrassing. You don't just knock on a fire station's door. It turns out you can. And you undoubtedly will when your mom instinct starts overpowering your ego.

As I reached the station's back door, I could see the firefighters all gathered for a meal. Promptly, someone came to the door, and before I knew it, I blurted it all out like a crazy lady: *My son is not responding! Something is wrong! We live right next door! Can you help?*

And let me tell you, in a matter of seconds there was a complete mission formed. Those guys literally brought the fire truck out of the garage and unloaded a huge ladder. They were ready to bust in our front door if needed. But first, they climbed up the ladder to my son's window.

And just as the firefighters almost reached his bedroom window, my son popped out on the balcony . . . staring at all of us like we were crazy people! Turns out, he had fallen into a deep sleep, with his headphones on, and his phone on do not disturb.

I was so embarrassed. And I think the first words out of my mouth were, "I'm going to kill him." Then I decided that was probably not a good idea in front of a bunch of first responders—

That's okay. This is what we do.

plus, I didn't want a visit from Child Protective Services.

I could not get over how quickly those firefighters jumped into action. I looked at them half embarrassed and half thankful and just said, "I'm so sorry." One of them looked at me and said something like, "That's okay. This is what we do." I haven't stopped thinking about that day and those words.

While I was living next door to the station, I saw firsthand the work that firefighters do each day to prep and train for the next emergency. They wash the fire truck, they roll out the hoses, they check their equipment, they play basketball and bond as a team.

And why? So they can be prepared for the next crisis. Because that is their calling. That is what they do.

THIS IS HOW WE CHANGE THE WORLD

I began this book by telling you how I wanted to "end missions." But the truth is, it's less about ending missions and more about breathing new life into it. A new kind of mission for a new kingdom people. One that speaks more to our desire to see God's kingdom come to life here on earth rather than our desire for the number of souls saved. A mission that believes in HELP and HOPE. A mission that doesn't get lost in the either/or. A mission that embraces both.

> **True transformation isn't a set of equations, and hope isn't a formula.**

I have seen that kind of missions. I have lived it, breathed it, tasted it, and more than anything, I want you to see it too.

But how exactly do we do that? Where do we even start?

The catch is, there's no one-size-fits-all for missions. True transformation isn't a set of equations, and hope isn't a formula.

Every place is different. Every community has its own unique set of challenges and strengths. And every Christ-follower has something crucial to contribute.

I don't have any prescriptions or how-tos. That's where the beauty of both comes in. There's room for all of it—room for you, room for your ideas, your passions, your imagination, your people. But here are a few things I've learned along the way.

1. GIVE UP YOUR HONEY

I was in Rwanda visiting one of the most remote locations I have ever seen. This was a community living in extreme poverty. They had the highest concentration of HIV/AIDS in all of Rwanda—yet, no medical resources. This was also a place where children were abandoned. Parents would leave to find work, never to return. There were children everywhere I looked.

One of our donors had provided a much-needed church building for this community, and I had the privilege of handing out Bibles to people who had never owned one. I wish I could describe their excitement—how they rushed to line up and filled the church to receive their own copy of God's Word. In spite of their desperate conditions, God's Word was still precious to them.

After we finished the distribution, I walked by a bench where a young girl sat holding her new Bible, excitedly reading it to her friend. It made me even more grateful for the opportunity to minister to these people.

We spent the entire day at this village—it was hot, dusty, dirty. And I was tired, hungry, and to be honest, emotionally spent. We loaded the car and were ready to leave. I cleaned off my hands and arms to hold me until I could get a good shower. But then one of our team members came to my window and said the village pastor wanted me to come to his home and pray over him and his family.

Now, I would like to say my immediate reaction was sweet and spiritual. But it was not. I reluctantly dragged myself out of the car. But soon the heat and hunger disappeared as I stood before this dedicated pastor and his extended family in their modest home. And I realized he wanted me—*me*—to pray over him. I was humbled, I was convicted. Then they proceeded to present me with a gift. It was in a bag, but inside I could see a jerry can. You know, those bright yellow jugs we see in photos of people carrying water in Africa.

What would happen if we all "gave up our honey" in the same way?

I did not want to be rude, so I waited to open it until we got back to the car. What could this be? Did he give me a jug of water? Was it cooking oil? To my surprise, it was honey—the largest jug of honey I've ever held, and I'm sure the most valuable thing they could have given me.

This pastor—who shepherds a flock in so much need; who, along with his family, lives a life of extreme poverty—had given me the very best of what they had. And I will never forget.

To some people, that village in Rwanda was a picture of scarcity. But I know personally it was a land flowing with milk and honey.

And it makes me wonder, what precious gift do you have to give to the world? What skills, passions, and resources are unique to you and only you? And what would happen if we all put our best gifts forward with the same joy and expectancy?

What would happen if we all "gave up our honey" in the same way?

2. PLANT SEEDS OF HOPE

One of my visits to Zambia was during its winter season, but it was not the kind of winter I knew. With temperatures ranging between 41 degrees and 75 degrees (F.), Zambia's winter requires a jacket in the morning and evening—but has you ripping it off midday.

I was introduced to Bruce and Malika, a husband and wife who lived with their three children along a long, dusty road. If I'm honest, I thought this was just another family living in extreme poverty, struggling to survive amidst a pandemic that was tearing the world apart. But I could not have been more wrong.

Bruce spoke with a sense of pride and passion that was truly inspiring. Behind him stood his modest house in desperate need of some major repairs. But you would never have known that from Bruce. To him, he was standing in front of a beautiful castle or mansion—a place that was his, and one he was proud to call home.

This family is part of a community struggling most days to find food and feed their children. Work is scarce, and educating your children, a luxury. And then a global pandemic hit, simply making a bad situation worse.

But that was before help and hope dared to show up in this almost forgotten part of the world. Right across the street from Bruce and Malika's home is an Empowerment Center supported by the World Help family. This center has allowed Malika to be part of a women's co-op group. They garden together to help provide food for this rural Zambian community as well as earn an income.

Malika and her husband shared how much the Empowerment Center has helped them as a family. They have learned about raising crops and rabbits, solar power, irrigation systems, and so much more that is providing them a sustainable way of life. They are raising twelve rabbits, have a beautiful garden, and enjoy their own water well—which means their children don't have to cross the dangerous road to fetch water somewhere else.

They were so grateful for the help from the center. "As women, we have been empowered to utilize the land," Malika shared. And Bruce added, "People see Jehovah through the helping hand."

The World Help family has provided a great deal for this community: food, blankets, books, clean water, and so much more. Elizabeth, the village headwoman, thanked us for sending relief. "Please don't stop," she said, "I'm looking after so many people—elderly, disabled, and blind. Thank God, He brought you here."

But it's not just the supplies that have made a difference in this community. Bruce and Malika are an example of what can be, and what is possible for others like them. And when you believe something that seems impossible is possible . . . well, that is hope.

What happened next is a moment forever etched in my memory. Malika walked up and gave me a simple little plant, so small you could not yet tell what it would become. She wanted me to plant it outside the Empowerment Center in honor of our visit. I found out it was a lemon tree. A lemon tree that would one day produce beautiful fruit.

I read that a lemon tree was considered a sign of hope by the early Christians. Hope for the future.

Even though that little lemon tree will take some time to produce fruit, the seeds of help have been planted. And the hope for a better future has been envisioned—a future full of empowered families.

> Hope is all about a future we can't yet see ...

You see, it's not just about handouts . . . or food . . . or clean water . . . or a rabbit. It's about help and hope. It's about how our lives change when we have it and how they are destroyed without it.

Hope is all about a future we can't yet see—a lemon tree that has yet to bear fruit. And it requires a long-term investment in something we believe is possible. Overnight results are great. But more often than not, true transformation takes time and commitment.

What issues are you passionate about solving? What is the beautiful future you see? And do you have what it takes to make the long-term investment needed to see those things become a reality? We are not just talking about money here, although that is important. We are talking about patience, commitment, emotional stamina, and never wavering in our faith.

It's about looking at what's in your hands, right here, right now. It's not about being perfect or performing grand gestures. It's about planting signs of hope for all the world to see—seed by seed, one by one.

3. FIND YOUR PEOPLE

I've always loved this quote by Mr. Rogers: "When I was a boy and would see scary things in the news, my mother would say to me, 'look for the helpers. You will always find people who are helping.'"[1] I often share this when I have the chance to speak about World Help.

During one event, I stood before an audience wearing a bright yellow vest. Why? Because we can all visualize first responders wearing something that sets them apart as "helpers." And in many cases, it is a bright yellow vest. We see it during news coverage of humanitarian crises around the world. We see it in our own neighborhoods as children are shepherded across the street by crossing guards. And yes, you even see them at your local Chick-fil-A drive thru!

But why do they wear them? Because these vests are a visible example of who they are and what they do. To someone in desperate need, the vest is a sign of help and hope. That night, I stood in front of that room of helpers and issued them their own uniforms.

In a matter of seconds, the entire ballroom was full of people wearing bright yellow vests. A few sheepishly and even reluctantly pulled theirs on, but it was a sight to behold. I asked the audience to take a minute and look around, soak it all in. Some even started taking pictures and videos of the moment.

I asked the crowd to take the vests home, and if they wanted to wear them around the house, go right ahead! But, in all serious-

1 Fred Rogers and Barry Head, *Mr. Rogers Talks to Parents* (Berkley Books, June 1, 1983).

ness, I hoped they would place the vests somewhere that would catch their eye every now and then. And when that happened, I wanted them to remember who they are and what they do. Who we are together and what we do together.

As I looked out over the room, I told them I saw a room full of helpers—first responders to a world in need.

But the truth is, what I see goes way beyond that room. The body of Christ is full of helpers. It's who we are. It is what we do. Isn't that who the church is supposed to be to a hurting world? Isn't that what people of faith do?

> We can be on the front lines, first responders to the world's greatest needs.

And as first responders, we can make sure that when the next Afghanistan or Ukraine refugee crisis happens, we will already be on the ground helping people survive.

When a pastor in a persecuted country runs out of Bibles, we can make sure we have the supplies to fill that urgent request.

When the next big hurricane devastates people's lives and homes, we can make sure we rush aid in and be the first on the ground, even before the dust settles.

When a virus and lockdowns leave people hungry and starving, we can be there to feed people and meet their most basic needs.

We can continue to provide help for today and hope for tomorrow.

We can be on the front lines, first responders to the world's greatest needs.

And you know what makes helpers even more powerful? A room full of them. A community working together toward the same goal, common vision, and shared passion. A team.

My youngest son is now in college playing baseball. But, when he was still a little guy, we lived the travel baseball life. You baseball parents know. Long weekends spent at a not-so-great hotel, scrubbing the red dirt out of your son's white uniform pants in the hotel laundry room. Either freezing or sweating during games, and eating your meals at concession stands. And believe it or not, I miss those days.

At one of those many tournaments, I found myself trying to watch the game from the warmth of my car. It was a cold, rainy, and really miserable day. We were playing a team from another state that we had never played before. We knew little about them or their players, and they knew little about us.

My son, Bentley, was about 9 or 10 at the time, and he was our lead-off hitter. In the first inning, he walked to the plate with a new bat my husband had just bought him. He had never hit with it before, never played a game with it. A little risky, but that is Bentley's style. He is "all in," every minute of every game.

The pitcher for the other team was huge for his age and was throwing "heat" as they say.

First pitch – ball.
Second pitch – ball.
Third pitch – strike.
Fourth pitch – foul ball; strike two.
And then something magical happened.

On the fifth pitch, Bentley swung that bat, made contact, and started running. He was by far the fastest kid on our team and could round those bases so quickly you would almost miss it. He didn't care where the ball went; he just tried to get on base. That's the job of the lead-off hitter—just get on base.

As he was approaching first base, he looked up just in time to see his ball flying over the fence and realized he had hit a home run. And not just any home run, but his very *first* home run. His run turned into a slow stride as he savored the moment of which every little boy dreams.

But here is the in-teresting part. The other team did not know this was his first home run. For all they knew, Bentley hit a home run every time he was up to bat.

> My prayer is that when confronted with the big needs of our world, people would say, "Back up! Back up!"

So, for the rest of the game, whenever he was up to bat, the other team got ready. The players scrambled and the coaches would start yelling, "Back up! Back up!"

My prayer is that when confronted with the big needs of our

world, people would say, "Back up! Back up!" The church is up to bat. People of faith are up to bat. Christ-followers are up to bat. The World Help family is up to bat.

Something big is about to happen. Back up! Malnourished babies are going to be rescued, people will have access to clean water, persecuted believers will have Bibles, the sick will receive medical attention. Lives are going to be transformed, the hopeless will have hope.

That is the kind of church the world needs right now. That is what people of faith should be known for. Not a people divided over the either/ors of life but united in the power of *both*.

> ... more than anything, I just want you in the game.

We need to be the people the world is looking to, not the ones sitting on the sidelines. With whom can you lock arms? Look specifically for ones who are passionate about solving the same problems as you. Find the people who are already helping. And if you are still looking, I have just the community for you—World Help. There's really nothing like it that I've found in all my years of "missions work." But more than anything, I just want you in the game.

BOTH WILL CHANGE THE WORLD

"This was their finest hour."[2] You most likely remember these words from Winston Churchill. Just six weeks in office as Britain's Prime Minister—and threatened with a Nazi invasion—

2 Churchill, Winston. "This was their finest hour," speech to House of Commons, United Kingdom. June 18, 1940.

Churchill gave what is considered even now as one of the greatest speeches ever delivered. In the face of a crisis that literally threatened the entire world, he said, "If the British Empire . . . lasts for a thousand years, men will still say, 'This was their finest hour.'"

It is said this speech rallied British morale because it helped people understand what they were fighting for—and that the hope of so much of the world rested on their shoulders.

I believe this could be our finest hour.

Just like generations before us, our stories will be shared, and history will remember us by our actions during our own global crises—by what we choose to do, or what we choose not to do.

And I believe the history of people of faith and the stories of the lives we impact around the world will be written—by what we choose to do or not to do.

And, in the midst of some of the greatest crises of our generation, I, too, believe this could be our finest hour.

We can choose to believe the whole truth: there is suffering in this world.

That sorrow and injustice and indifference do surround us.

That so many people simply choose to look away from the pain of their brothers and sisters.

And yet . . . the truth is, there is also goodness.

There is kindness and courage and radical, messy, ordinary love.

Every single person is made in the image of God—even our enemies. Because of this image, and God's grace, we have the capacity to do good in this world.

Because the world may change. But our mission will not. This, after all, is what we do.

The Message version of 1 John 4: 20-21 says our love of God is tied to our love for our neighbors. "If anyone boasts, 'I love God,' and goes right on hating his brother or sister, thinking nothing of it, he is a liar. If he won't love the person he can see, how can he love the God he can't see? The command we have from Christ is blunt: loving God includes loving people. You've got to love both."

> **The world may change. But our mission will not. This, after all, is what we do.**

For our love to be real to God, we have to love our neighbors.

We've got to love both.

For our strategies to be effective, we have to meet people's physical and spiritual needs.

We've got to love both.

For earth to start looking a little more like heaven, we have to give Help for today. And we have to give Hope for tomorrow.

God is interested in both.

In a world fighting between either/or and us vs. them, "both" can change the world.

Because "both" is what we do.

 Scan the QR code for photos, videos, and more details about the stories from around the world shared in this chapter.

WorldHelp®
Help for today. **Hope** for tomorrow.

World Help is a Christian humanitarian organization serving the physical and spiritual needs of people in impoverished communities around the world.

It's our desire to see God's kingdom come to life here on earth. And for earth to start looking a little more like heaven, we have to give both Help for today ... and Hope for tomorrow. In a world fighting between either/or and us vs. them, "both" can change the world.

World Help works with national partners around the globe to plant churches, provide clean water to communities, ship lifesaving aid to disaster victims, rescue girls trapped in the sex industry, pull children out of poverty, help refugees, send Bibles worldwide, and more.

You can join us! Become a world changer today and discover how the power of HELP and HOPE can transform everything.

Learn more and get involved at worldhelp.net.

ACKNOWLEDGMENTS

Years ago there was a magazine I loved called *Need*. It highlighted humanitarian work around the world. But what I loved most was the slogan. On every inside cover were the words, "We are not out to save the world, but to tell the stories of those who do."

That is exactly how I feel about this book. I am telling the stories of people who are changing the world—from our World Help team and family of supporters to our partners on the ground doing the work day in and day out. And it is the people we serve whose stories of courage, determination, and faith inspire me every day.

But I hope we can do both—to continue to tell these incredible stories faithfully and authentically and, in doing so, inspire others to get involved; to witness more lives changed and communities transformed, to tell the stories and change the world. To do both.

And there are so many who have contributed to this story.

I want to especially thank Suzanne O'Dell, my content developer and editor. We have worked together for years, and there is no one who better understands my heart. She helps me get on paper what I want to express in a more authentic and compelling way. Suzanne, your wisdom, insight, and beautiful lens through which you see the world are woven throughout these pages. I literally could not have completed this book without you, and I am forever grateful.

Lauren, the title "assistant" does not accurately describe all that you do. This book reflects your tenacity, heart, and passion to help me accomplish so much more than I ever could on my own. I am so blessed to work with you.

Joanna, thank you for such a beautiful cover design. You are extremely talented, and you captured the meaning of "both" in a creative and inspiring way.

To our Communications team—Amanda, Rachel, Megan, Aly, Erin, and Ryan. Thank you for your patience through countless revisions and changes. Through your editing, design, and marketing plans, you brought this book to life in so many ways.

To our International Partnerships team, Kraig and Joseph. Thank you for helping me tell these stories in a way that honors our partners and the people they serve.

To my executive team, Allyn and Chad. I am so proud of the way you lead World Help. Thank you for allowing me the space to focus on this project.

To my dad, Vernon Brewer. You didn't just tell me about the needs of the world, you showed me and took me on the journey with you. And because of that, your passion became my passion. Thank you.

And to the World Help family, you demonstrate the power of both every day. I hope I have shared our story well.

ABOUT THE AUTHOR

Noel Brewer Yeatts is president of World Help, a Christian humanitarian organization serving the physical and spiritual needs of people in impoverished communities around the world. World Help gives help for today and hope for tomorrow through humanitarian aid and relief, community development, education and sustainability projects, Bible distribution, and church planting.

Noel was named president in 2019, having served for more than two decades in various aspects of the organization's humanitarian work. During her tenure, Noel has not only led through the pandemic, but also has spearheaded World Help's refugee crisis work in Afghanistan and Ukraine, as well as fought for victims of modern slavery and sex trafficking. Noel has a passion to change the face of missions, to breathe new life into it, and to invite people of faith into a new kind of kingdom work.

A frequent speaker at conferences and churches, Noel is also the author of several books including *Awake: Doing a World of Good, One Person at a Time.*

When Noel is not traveling the world, she loves spending time with her husband, Patrick; her two adult sons, Riley and Bentley; and her dog, Thunder. She lives in Lynchburg, Virginia, near World Help's headquarters. Learn more at www.worldhelp.net/bothbook.